A JOURNEY TO
RECOVERY
Speak Sobriety

STEPHEN HILL

with MARC HOBERMAN

Published by Speak Sobriety LLC

ISBN 978-0-692-95131-6

Cover design by Judith S Design & Creativity
www.judithsdesign.com

Contact Stephen Hill at shill@speaksobriety.com

Visit Stephen Hill's website at speaksobriety.com

Follow Stephen on social media @speaksobriety

Stephen Hill is available for speaking engagements, treatment planning and intervention consultations.

In loving memory of all of those who have lost their lives to the disease of addiction and substance abuse.

Port Chester Middle School, January 2018.

Gill St. Bernard's School, November 2017.

Which brother has the disease of addiction?

PROLOGUE

Waking up in a two-story suite overlooking the Atlantic Ocean at the Tropicana Casino & Resort in Atlantic City certainly has its advantages. In fact, the suite cost me nothing, and yet it cost me everything. My host at the Tropicana took good care of me. I was treated as if I were a celebrity. This experience was anything but free, and I would have preferred to wake up in my own bed in Suffern, New York, a suburb 30 miles north of New York City.

As I awoke on the floor of my hotel room, my eyes fell upon a pile of my own vomit. This was the result of a night of self-destruction: countless hours snorting lines of OxyContin and cocaine, drinking Red Bull and vodka, chain smoking Marlboro Lights, and playing $1,000 hands of blackjack. At that moment, the luxury of my suite paled in comparison to the debauchery that occurred fewer than 24 hours earlier. I may have overdosed that night; I cannot be sure. The image that I saw in the mirror was a multicolored palette that I had never seen before. My bloodshot eyes lost their natural blue color. My skin, a greenish yellow shade supplanted a black and blue welt on my head. In an effort to ensure that I would never repeat that awful experience, I promised myself that I would no longer mix substances and would simply stick to my drug of choice, OxyContin. At the time, that was the best anyone could hope for.

A week earlier, I had turned 23. It wasn't a birthday bash with celebration and presents; nobody would feel like celebrating on such a day. I had lost $10,000 playing blackjack at the Wynn Casino in Las Vegas. I was with my girlfriend at the time, and soon after my loss, I proceeded to rip lines of Oxy right in front of her. She called Oxy my mistress; I called it my savior. She said that for me, Oxy came before everything, and she could not have been more right. She ended our relationship that night, and of course I can't blame her. Many things began and ended that evening.

I was not a novice to nights such as these. For some, these nights are the exception, but for me, they were the norm. The danger and chaos of drug use and the criminal lifestyle that came with it made me feel alive, but dead inside at the same time. My mistress had me under the spell of a magical substance that I believed would help me rule the world. Even as a child, I was known as a risk taker. I looked forward to the night before Halloween all year long. We called it Gate Night. My friends and I would run the streets late at night causing trouble. Every year I took my mischief to a new level. As I reflect on my youth, I ask myself, "How does a 6-year-old running into the lake in the middle of winter on a dare become a young adult who makes life and death decisions on a daily basis?" One might think that I am the "typical" drug addict, raised in a low-income family with a history of parental drug abuse; not so. There wasn't any traumatic event in my life that led me down this destructive path. I come from a good family, a great family in fact. I was athletic, had many friends, dated girls, and did well in school. Everything seemed to be perfect in my personal bubble. My parents raised three other sons who never had any of the problems that I encountered. So, what happened? Something went wrong, very wrong. It is almost impossible to know how this descent began, but it is all too easy to recall the physical, emotional, and financial destruction that I caused in less than a decade.

After several years of drug use, illegal activity, and unsuccessful stays at a multitude of rehabilitation facilities, I have emerged as a proponent of sobriety instead of another deadly statistic. I believe that my rise from the abyss to the surface will resonate with people who can learn from my mistakes. My story has already affected the lives of thousands of people. For me, this memoir is a sojourn of the heart. This is the story of my journey to recovery.

INTRODUCTION

Addiction turned me into someone that I am not and made me do things that I would not normally do, and I suffered great consequences because of my addiction. I pass along the message of consequences each time I share my story at a middle school, high school, college, community forum, or support group. But, my battle with substance abuse has also made me the man I am today.

Sobriety is about much more than simply being sober. Sobriety is about being a good person, helping other people, doing the next right thing, and chasing your dreams. If I am able to stay clean and sober one day at a time after a decade of substance abuse, then others can as well.

Almost every time I speak, a student will ask me after my presentation, "If you could go back and change one thing, what would you change?" In October of 2016, I was asked this question by a student at Garfield High School in Bergen County, New Jersey; however, this student took the question to the next level when he heard my response and added, "If you did change that one thing and you never had any of these struggles, then you would not be here speaking to us today." This statement made me pause and reflect on those words and what my story could mean to others.

In recovery, I have been taught to never regret the past, but to also never shut the door on it. There was an enormous amount of collateral damage that affected my friends and family as a result of my substance abuse which I can never erase.

Just as sports was my identity throughout my childhood, drugs became my identity in my teens and early twenties. However, sobriety is my identity today, and it is now the most exciting time of my life. Everything good that I have in my life today is a direct result of sobriety. To answer that student's question, I would change the harm that my addiction caused other people, but I am who I am today because of my addiction, so for that, I will be eternally grateful.

Although I truly believe I am in a place of great strength and passion today, I would not wish addiction on my worst enemy. I was able to escape alive, but certainly not unscathed. I know too many people who have destroyed or even lost their lives as a result of drugs and alcohol. The truth is, even one is too many.

This is why I share my story. I have been praised by thousands of people for having the courage to speak openly and honestly about my struggles with addiction. Public speaking came naturally to me, and many believe that I have a compelling and powerful tale to tell. I still can feel my heart pounding out of my chest each time I present, but I breathe easy, take a sip of water, and hit the stage. Once the microphone is in my hand, it's game time. I believe it is my duty as a sober man to use my experiences to help others. If sharing my story can help just one person every time I speak, or help just one person who reads this book, then I have accomplished my mission and fulfilled my purpose.

CHAPTER 1
Background Check

If you talk to any of my close friends or family, they will tell you that I have one of the best memories of anyone they have ever known. For some reason, I can recall the most vivid details about events that took place during my childhood. When a friend or family member is struggling to remember details about a certain event or story, they call on me to fill in the blanks. In my life, this is both a blessing and a curse. I love to remember the good times, but there was a dark period in my life that I often wish I could forget. Other than the nights I was abusing Xanax, which was not very often, I can still remember the details that encompassed the insanity of my disease.

Let me be clear, my memory only works this way for past experiences. I cannot read a chapter in a book and remember everything word for word. I am lucky if I comprehend half of what I read. That awesome memory gene was bestowed upon my older brother, Michael...Mike. He's the smartest one in the family, and one of the most intelligent people I know. He loves to read and did exceptionally well in school. Although I come from a family of lawyers who love to argue, we all agree that Mike is the smartest. He went on to graduate Magna Cum Laude from Georgetown University and Fordham University School of Law. Today, he lives in Brooklyn with his wife, Camy, and his son, Oliver, and works at a very successful law firm in Manhattan.

Mike was born 16 months before me on Long Island in New York. My father grew up in Baldwin, also on Long Island. He was living there with my mother to be along with my father's big Irish Catholic family. Kevin

Hill, my father, has three sisters and two brothers. All of them have the gene that torments my family, the disease of addiction. My grandfather was no exception. My father and grandmother, Elaine, were the only two in their family who never had a problem with drugs or alcohol. By the grace of God, all of my father's siblings are sober today. My grandfather, Jake, passed away in 2008 a kind, decent, and sober man.

My dad met my mom in college at SUNY Oneonta. My mom's best friend since childhood, Sharon Kubart, who attended the same college, introduced them. They married young, just a few years out of college. My dad is an amazing athlete, and his chosen sport was baseball. He had a tryout with the New York Mets, but didn't make the team.

When it came to all aspects of life, my dad was a focused and driven individual. He didn't have a lot of money growing up and really wanted to make something of himself. Even though Mike and I were already part of the family, my dad decided to go to law school at the age of 29. My mom pushed him and gave her full support, and it was one of the best decisions they ever made. My dad graduated from St. John's Law School in 1992. He got a job straight out of law school working for IBM, and he has been an attorney there for over 25 years. He didn't take the job at a big law firm because he wanted to be around for his family. He coached me and all of my brothers at one time or another. When we had to be driven to a 6:00a.m. ice hockey game, he was most often the one behind the wheel.

Shortly before I was born, my parents decided to move to Suffern, New York to be around my mother's family. My mother, Laurie, lived in Suffern her entire life and still lives there today. She was a computer programmer at Nautica when we were younger, and then went to work for DKNY. She was one of the first telecommuters of her generation which allowed her to work from home a good amount of the time. My mom did everything for us. She cooked our favorite meals, did pickups and drop-offs at school, drove us to practices and games, helped with homework, was involved in the school PTA, and volunteered a lot of her free time fundraising for our sports teams, all while working a full-time job.

Through good times and bad, my mom never gave up on me. She stood by me through some of the most awful times in my life. Some might consider her devotion towards the end of my addiction as enabling, but no one can fathom what it is like to be the parent, especially the mother of a drug addict unless they have gone through it themselves.

The Bartolomucci's, my mother's family, are Italian. Almost no one pronounces the name correctly. I think my mom was relieved to lose 8 letters and change her last name to Hill. My grandparents on my mother's side, Ella and Mario Bartolomucci played a major role in my childhood. My parents would drop me and my brothers off at their house before they went to work. My grandfather, Mario, was an extremely hard worker. He was involved in various businesses but made most of his money with his food trucks. In his leisure time, Mario was a magician. The best part of his magic tricks was not when they were perfectly executed, but when things went horribly wrong and he tried to cover it up. He once gave an exploding magic marker to my friend. It was only supposed to make a small pop, but it blew up in my friend's face. You could smell the scent of his burning eyebrows as my grandfather quickly ran out of the room. In 2007, my grandfather passed away from Parkinson's disease.

We affectionately call my grandmother, Nana. She sold her house and built an addition onto my parents' house when my grandfather became ill. She has been living with us since 2006. I call her wing of the house the West Wing, which is the forbidden wing in *Beauty and the Beast.* Others refer to it as the right wing, since Fox News is on all morning, noon, and night.

Nana gets along very well with my father's mother, Elaine. The way they keep the peace is to never talk politics; Elaine is as liberal as they come. Grandma Elaine has a big heart, dreamy imagination, and is extremely well-informed. Even while battling cancer, she still manages to stay up to date on the hot topics of the day. Too many people have mistaken Grandma Elaine's kindness for weakness. If you are a right wing conservative and try to push your views onto her, get ready for an all-out brawl with an extremely knowledgeable and outspoken grandma. My aunt Eileen witnessed a heated argument between Grandma Elaine and a few conservatives while they were all receiving chemotherapy. At least they were all able to take their minds off cancer for a short period of time.

Nana is the best cook around. I am sure there are many people who believe the same about their grandmothers, but this is not a biased opinion: it's a fact. She brought out a gigantic dish of over 100 meatballs at my mother's 50th birthday celebration; they were gone in a matter of minutes. Her meatloaf with caramelized onions or eggplant parmigiana with spaghetti are the two best dishes I have ever eaten. Nana pretends to be willing to share her recipes and techniques with the rest of the family, but that is not really true. When you ask her how long the eggplant should be cooked, her response is usually, "Until it's done! You think I need a measuring cup or timer at this point? I know how much to put in and how long to put it in for. Figure it out yourself!"

Nana has quite the social life for an 89-year-old woman. She plays in two different games of Mah-Jongg. This is as entertaining for me as it is for her. Her active lifestyle enables me to get up to the minute grandma gossip. "Lauretta is always late, Eileen talks too much, Lenore is the best person I know." On Saturday nights, she goes out with the girls. Nana is also a die hard Mets fan. She screams, "You jerks," and yells at the television when the Mets aren't performing well. When they are winning, she claps as if she is at the game.

If it were up to Nana, every family member would come to the house for Sunday dinner regardless of other responsibilities. Although these are fond memories, Nana is the matriarch of our family, and I am saddened that she was forced to witness the consequences of my drug addiction.

On September 19, 1987, I was born at Good Samaritan Hospital. My Uncle Rich Reimer was watching my brother Mike while my mom was in labor and the rest of the family was at the hospital. Rich was dating my mom's older sister, Joanne, whom we affectionately call Jojo. That night, Rich was cooking something on the stove when Mike took it upon himself to give him a nickname that would last a lifetime, "Cook." We still call him that to this day.

We were very close with the Reimers growing up, and still are. My cousin Julie was born two years after me. She was more like a sister than a cousin. Julie's sister Stephanie and my brother Johnny came next in 1991 and were born just 6 months apart.

My mom says Johnny was the sweetest baby and child growing up. He got a lot tougher by the time he was in high school and is presently one of the most strong-willed and hardest working people I know. He is also extremely intelligent. Johnny is finishing his last semester at Brooklyn Law School and will also be working at a very successful law firm in Manhattan, just like Mike.

When it comes to book smarts, I can't compete with my brothers Johnny or Michael, nor do I want to. My brothers and I all pride ourselves on never being jealous of one another, admiring each of our individual talents. I love throwing brain busters at Mike. I once asked him a question I was sure would stump him. To add insult to injury, not only did he have the correct answer, it turns out I didn't even know the right answer when I asked the question.

It was 1995 and my parents had three boys. They wanted a girl, so they gave it one last shot. Yet again, another boy. Kevin Hill, Jr. was born on April 19, 1996. We called him KJ as a baby, and now it's just K. Not exactly a time saver, but if the letter fits, and it does, wear it.

K was the proverbial kid who was ahead of his time. That often happens when you have three older brothers. He knew way too much about life for his age. He knew what pot smelled like when he was 6 years old. Whenever I would come home stoned he would say, "Steve, you smell like pot." K always wanted to be included when we played sports or video games. At the age of 4 he started playing video games, but his hands were too small for the PlayStation and Nintendo 64 controllers. K wasn't going to allow his lack of size to keep him from playing. He made various adjustments with his hands, fingers, and the way he held the controller. He got so used to holding the controller in this way that he stuck with it well after his hands were big enough to hold the controller normally.

Of all the Hill boys, my mom says that K was the most difficult as a baby. A crier. He threw two epic temper tantrums that will be forever etched in our memories. One was at the Major League Baseball Hall of Fame in Cooperstown, New York when he found out he had to return the baby New York Yankees uniform he wore to have his picture taken. He screamed, cried, and tried his hardest to get out of my dad's grip. He fought so hard and screamed so loudly that tourists thought he was being kidnapped. We were with my best friend Conor Andreas' family at the time. Conor's two older brothers, Matt and Ryan, babysat for K and gave it their best shot to calm him down. At the end of the day, we all failed. Luckily fatigue set in and K passed out.

He did the same thing when we walked out of a movie at the Palisades Mall and passed KB Toys. He wanted a new WWE action figure, but my parents didn't exactly share his enthusiasm. He even opened the car door on the New York State Thruway when we were on the way home. A young boy willing to risk his life for a WWE action figure. Now that's commitment!

I built a mini hockey arena in our basement when I was in 8th grade. K was only 4 or 5 years old and played in games and tournaments with us. This is where he learned to stick handle and hold a puck like a professional hockey player. K was the superstar Suffern Hockey player. He was part of the New York State championship Suffern Hockey team his sophomore year. His junior year he was the leading scorer and made first team all-state. He was the leading scorer and captain of the team his senior year, and the Rockland County Player of the Year. He went on to repeat his senior year of high school at Kent Prep in Connecticut. This is a common strategy hockey players use in order to get noticed. He ended up playing Division 3 hockey at Wesleyan University. He recently transferred to Boston College and is now focused on a career in investment banking. He also plays on the club hockey team there.

Every time I have a speaking engagement and share my story, I say, "My brothers and I all grew up in the same house, with the same family, played the same sports, and had the same type of friends. As kids, we pretty much did everything the same. So why was I the only one with the drug problem?" The only way for me to answer that question is to say that I was born with the disease of addiction. When I take that first drink or that first drug, I cannot stop. My disease will force me to use more, to progress to harder drugs, and to do whatever is necessary to maintain my addiction; whatever is necessary.

My addiction manifested itself early. Others make it through high school, or even college, and then start to see problems into their twenties or later. You cannot understand how powerful the disease of addiction really is unless you have experienced it for yourself. For someone who hasn't experienced drug addiction, think of your drug of choice as food and water. You need food and water to survive and you cannot live without it. When you are addicted to drugs such as OxyContin or heroin, it completely consumes your life. If you run out of your drug of choice, it's like running out of food and water. The drug becomes as important as oxygen to a human being or water to a fish.

The media shames drug offenders in the news daily. They post our mugshots in the paper and on the news, exposing us for the horrible things we did. I even see community coalition members who claim to be addiction advocates making Facebook posts about the stigma attached to the disease of addiction one day, and then posting the mug shot of a nonviolent drug offender the next. Do you see a problem there? I do. Many times, I see drug addicts being charged with petty larceny. In plain English, that's stealing. If you or your loved ones were starving and you had no money to buy food, would you steal? Of course, it is wrong, but being addicted to drugs is like starving all the time, and the only way to keep yourself from withering away is to "feed" your addiction. That is the goal: to get high, and stay high.

CHAPTER 2
Cook Saw the Recipe for Disaster

I am often asked the question by parents, "Looking back, were there any early warning signs that you or your parents now recognize?" K was the most difficult baby, but he never had any of the problems that I did. Some studies point to children who exhibit risk taking behavior and who are diagnosed with Attention Deficit Hyperactivity Disorder (ADHD) as higher risk candidates for substance abuse issues. I fall into both of these categories. Some studies also link depression and social anxiety to substance abuse disorders.

When I was 6 years old, my family got together at Lake Antrim in Suffern, New York. My best friend, Conor, lives on the lake. Lake Antrim was chosen as a meeting spot before we went out to dinner with family friends. It was in the middle of the winter of 1993, and one of the fathers thought it would be a brilliant idea to scream, "Last one in the lake is a rotten egg!" All seven kids ran towards the lake. Six out of the seven stopped just before the water; I ran right in. Everyone was laughing, except for my father. He was furious at me and even angrier with the adult who yelled out the challenge.

My father had to bring me home to change while everyone else headed to the restaurant. He asked me why I did it and I said that I didn't want to be the rotten egg. My father was no longer mad at me, but he realized then that I was different from the other kids.

My uncle Rich, who is also in recovery, said something to my father when I was only two years old. He said, "We are going to have to keep a close eye on that one." I was always bouncing off the walls and full of energy as a child. Although I had a lot of friends, was playing sports, and doing well in school, my ability to focus in the classroom became a problem in second grade. This was the first time I went to see a pediatric neurologist.

My parents took me to see Dr. Ronald Jacobson at Nyack Hospital in Rockland County. Dr. Jacobson was well-respected in the medical community. After running a few tests, Dr. Jacobson called my parents into the examining room and stated his diagnosis, Attention Deficit Hyperactivity Disorder. Inattention, hyperactivity, and impulsivity are the three main symptoms for a child who has ADHD. I exhibited all three symptoms but this was not the "hat trick" my family had expected.

Naturally, my parents asked, "Can it be treated, and if so, what is the treatment?" Dr. Jacobson immediately prescribed Ritalin, a central nervous system stimulant, which is a controlled substance. This sounded strange to my parents. My mother told me she remembers asking him why he would prescribe a stimulant to someone who already had trouble sitting still. She believed the medication would make me bounce off the walls even more.

For people who don't have ADHD, taking a stimulant would speed them up and make them ultra focused. For me, Ritalin did make me ultra focused, but it also turned me into a zombie. I understand that medication is necessary for some children who cannot focus and disrupt the classroom. Students like me often interfere with classroom instruction and make it difficult for teachers to maintain a proper learning environment.

I cannot help but think that there is something very wrong about prescribing a powerful stimulant to a seven-year-old. On top of that, I was also taking a mood stabilizer. My parents told me that alternative non-drug solutions weren't even discussed. If drugs can forever change the brain chemistry of an adult, what can it do to a seven-year-old? I cannot make this statement with any scientific certainty, but I believe that my exposure to a controlled substance at such a young age may have increased my vulnerability to addiction.

I hated the way Ritalin made me feel. I became a very quiet kid, had trouble socializing, and lost my appetite. Certainly, I wasn't the only child who was prescribed Ritalin or another stimulant. There was a line of young students at the nurse's office during lunch waiting to take their medication. In fact, two of them were my close friends. Our mother's confided in each other about their children's common struggles. I would sometimes go directly to recess to avoid taking my medication. Sure enough, one of the lunch monitors would come out and make me take my meds. Not only did I dislike the way the medication made me feel, I was also embarrassed about taking it in school at the nurse's office. My mom started putting the medication in my lunch bag so I did not have to go to the nurse's office, but then I would sometimes forget to take it altogether. It was a never ending battle.

The side effects of taking Ritalin were terrible, but the drug did help me focus. I was seeing a psychologist once a week as well. I did very well in school in second grade after I started taking Ritalin. I was part of the independent group in Mrs. D'adamo's class. This independent group consisted of the five smartest students. Mrs. D'adamo gave us more challenging assignments than the rest of the class, and the five of us worked together to complete our work.

It could have been Mrs. D'adamo's friendly nature or teaching style that prevented me from getting into trouble in her class. Whatever it was, it worked. The next two years, however, were a nightmare for me. In third and fourth grade, I was sent out of the room and into the hallway almost every day for behavioral issues. Even with these outbursts, I was still one of the top students in the class.

When I was in third grade, we had a multiplication competition. My teacher gave the class a certain period of time to finish all the problems. If you finished before the timer went off and answered all of the problems correctly, you got to go on a field trip to Friendly's for ice cream.

What I remember most about this competition was that I finished first and answered all of the questions correctly. I even beat the smartest girl in the school. Little did she know that I was on speed, running through these numbers like an adding machine at an accounting firm. If I were drug tested, she could have had me disqualified or at least had an asterisk put next to my name like Mark McGwire and Barry Bonds. Only later did baseball fans find out that their idols were juiced up when they achieved their home run records.

During my time at Viola Elementary School, I found my identity in sports. I played almost every organized sport offered. I began playing ice hockey and baseball before I was out of preschool. My dad had my older brother and me start early. We would practice hitting and fielding in the backyard and joined the Suffern Little League when we entered kindergarten.

Little League baseball was a commitment, but it pales in comparison to the demands of ice hockey. Mike and I started taking skating lessons when I was just three years old and Mike was four. My closest friend and hockey teammate was Colin. We were in the same classes from preschool through high school.

It was comforting to have a close friend and brother at all of my games and practices. Mike also had a good friend named Jason. We started playing in a house league at Sport-O-Rama, an ice rink which was a five-minute drive from our home. A house league just means you play in a league against local teams and every game would be at the same rink. Many kids started playing travel hockey right away, but none of my friends played travel hockey until we were in 6th grade. Travel hockey was much more competitive and enabled us to play in significantly more games.

It is a very serious commitment for parents to allow their child to play travel ice hockey. It means giving up weekends and traveling to different ice rinks all over the Northeast. We even went to tournaments in Canada.

I had a really close group of friends at Viola Elementary. We called ourselves "the six." I believe there were originally six friends in our group; then we added a seventh, but still called ourselves "the six." We were all very close. I played different sports with all of them.

When I was in 4th grade, Viola Elementary School hired two new gym teachers. One of the new teachers was Mr. Drab. He was a young, athletic, and ambitious coach who wasted no time bringing an amazing program to Viola. He helped build a program all the way up to the varsity level at Suffern High School.

Mr. Drab started an early morning lacrosse league before school. Grades 4 through 6 were split up into 6 teams. Early morning lacrosse was every Tuesday for the majority of the school year. Each team would play against a different team every week.

I was a baseball player, so I decided I wasn't going to play when the league started because baseball and lacrosse are held the same season. About a month in, I decided I was going to join the league. My friend, Walter, wasn't the most talented player, but he always had the latest equipment. He was the first one to get the Edge Ice, a lacrosse stick that soon skyrocketed in popularity. I followed Walter's lead and bought an Edge Ice as well. All of my friends were playing lacrosse, including the baseball players. I was an above average baseball player and made the all-star team a few years, but there were several other players who were better than me.

Within a few weeks of joining the lacrosse league, I started to get the hang of it. Before long, I was one of the best players in my grade. I ended up joining a travel team as well and started to become more adept at lacrosse. In the Tuesday morning league at Viola, I was the leading scorer for my grade every year.

Even with my struggles with ADHD, my childhood experience at Viola Elementary School coupled with my involvement in organized sports was amazing. Even better was my experience growing up in a neighborhood with numerous friends. We were always able to play pickup sports and games all day and night.

CHAPTER 3
Dreamland

Growing up, The Knolls at Ramapough, a 500-unit condominium, was my dreamland. The Knolls is divided into 8 courts, each named after a Native American tribe. I lived in Jumano Court. The Knolls has lots of grounds to play pickup sports and games. Baseball, soccer, football, manhunt, and capture the flag were just a few of our favorites. We used the concrete to play basketball and roller hockey. The Knolls has a playground, tennis courts, and community pool. We had what seemed like the biggest hill in the world just a 10-second walk from our house; this was great for sleigh-riding in the winter. We flew off huge jumps with our blow-up snow tubes and hid in forts to barricade ourselves from enemies during snowball fights.

The best part of growing up in the Knolls was having so many friends who lived in the development. We could instantly get a pickup game started. We never had to worry about getting rides from our parents since we all lived within walking distance of one another. We would ride our bikes going door to door gathering the troops for whatever sport or game we decided to play. Sometimes, we had too many kids to play and had to split up into different games. The Knolls was our own mini Olympic village.

A 500-unit condo was a paradise for trick or treaters on Halloween. People from all over Suffern would come to the Knolls on October 31st. We started off accompanied by our parents, but were on our own shortly thereafter. My friends and I would grab an empty pillow case and head out. We hit every single house in the development. I used to love coming across the lazy people who would leave a bucket of candy outside with a sign that read, "Please take one." I always took just one, then another one, and another one...

During the exciting summer months at the Knolls, my mom and our next-door neighbor, Rose, threw huge block parties. There was a DJ, water balloon tosses, volleyball, and a ton of food. The parties were a lot of fun and the excitement continued at the pool with the Knolls Olympics. We split up into different teams and competed against each other.

The first week after school was out, as well as the last few weeks of the summer, was my favorite time as a child. This was the time when everyone who went to day or sleep away camp was home with nothing to do. These times were a constant free for all.

We played outside from the early morning until it was time for dinner, then went back to our respective houses to eat. We waited for the sun to go down and then met at the Kensico Court dumpster in front of one of my friends' condo. This dumpster wasn't an ordinary garbage container; it was surrounded by a jagged edged brick wall which served as the jail for our only nighttime game, Manhunt.

More people showed up for Manhunt than any other sport or game. Friends who lived outside the Knolls would also come to play. Even girls came out to join in the fun. This included my first girlfriend, Stacey. She and I shared the same backyard so we got to see each other often. She and I became close friends in high school, but I lost touch with her a few years after. Stacey would be one of many close friends I would lose as a direct result of my drug addiction.

Manhunt would usually end around 10:30p.m. Most of the kids had curfews, although I didn't have anything formal. Mike and I would escort our younger brother, Johnny, home after manhunt, then go back and hang with the older kids who had later curfews, or no curfew at all. This is when the real games of mischief began.

I felt so cool hanging out with the older guys after Manhunt ended. Conor did not live in the Knolls, but he was at my house practically every day. He was one of the few kids my age who was allowed to hang out late. We would walk around the grounds of the Knolls, stop at the park with the sign at the entrance that read, "Closed at dusk". We thought we were really cool hanging out in a closed park. We talked, played charades, or a movie/actor game. One person would name an actor, then the next person would name a movie he or she was in. Then the next person would have to name a different actor in that movie, and so on.

We also played truth or dare. This was my first real encounter with mischievous behavior. I remember an older girl daring me to "ring and run" a doorbell of a house on the corner. I was nervous, but in an excited kind of way. This would be just the beginning of risky behavior that would increase tenfold as the years progressed. We picked the house of a grumpy man who always complained about us making too much noise during Manhunt.

The group I was with watched eagerly as I approached the house. They all had about a five second head start. I remember the older girl telling me, "You have to ring the bell a bunch of times to make sure you wake them up." I quietly made my way to the front door. My heart was pounding as I inched closer to the door. I had been running around all night, so I was already drenched in sweat. I reached for the doorbell and rang it like I was signaling a ship with morse code. I turned around and jetted for safety, trailing the rest of the group. I was so nervous and running so quickly that I ran right into a parked car. As my bad luck would have it, the car had an alarm, a really loud one.

Not only did I wake up the grumpy man that night, I also woke up the residents of Kensico Court. I rounded the corner and headed for the "Big Field" where the older kids played their pickup baseball games. I met up with the rest of the group and we laid in the grass for a few minutes. We laughed and shushed each other at the same time. After about a minute, the car alarm went off. We laid in the grass for a few more minutes and then felt safe enough to come out of our hiding spot. The older kids were giving me high-fives and congratulating me on my first successful ring and run. We decided to call it a night, and I ran back to my house with Mike and Conor.

I felt so alive that night. My adrenaline was rushing, and I was full of energy. I felt like I was on top of the world. I was drawn to this kind of feeling and fell in love with risk taking. Planning the risk, committing the act, then soaking up my win, talking about it over and over after I completed my mission. This feeling consumed me, but it would not be enough, not nearly enough.

After a while, I wasn't getting the same feeling from a ring and run. I had never been caught, but it just wasn't as exciting as it used to be. I needed something more and I found myself chasing that feeling.

The summer ended and my 5th grade school year began. That October would be my first experience with "Gate Night," the night before Halloween. Gate Night was going to give me back that feeling I so desperately wanted, but the stakes would be higher.

Looking back on it now, my behavior did set off bells, whistles, and bright blinking lights for someone who might be a person ripe for drug addiction. The risk was my drug, and the first time was the best. I enjoyed it the next few times after that, but it quickly lost its effect. I needed more to get the same feeling naturally or otherwise.

CHAPTER 4
It Happened for a Reason

Mrs. Wilson was Mike's fifth grade teacher, and my mother wanted me to be in her class as well. I ended up in a different class, but my mom went to the school and was able to get me switched. Mrs. Wilson had a no nonsense style of teaching, and I actually took very well to it. I never got in trouble and did very well that year.

That year, I participated in my first Gate Night. I have heard other people call the night before Halloween bad boys night, cabbage night, mischief night, devil's night and more. It came as no surprise that The Knolls was patrolled by private security on Gate Night and Halloween. I invited Conor to come over since his parents were the only other adults who would allow their younger children to go out on Gate Night. My parents let me, Conor, and Mike go out with a few rolls of toilet paper and silly string. Unbeknownst to my parents, I stole a carton of eggs from Nana's house that week in preparation for the night's festivities.

We started using the silly string on cars and wrapped toilet paper around the pine trees. About a half hour in, a security car spotted us and started driving towards us with his little yellow light blinking. We ran and got away. Then, I took out the carton of eggs I had hidden in the bushes. We each took 4 eggs and threw them against the brick sidewall of one of the condos. We ran back in the house and stayed in for the rest of the night. I couldn't sleep because I was so excited about my first successful Gate Night.

5th grade was a big year for me. Conor and I decided we were going to try to date older girls. Somehow, we found a pair of 7th grade best friends, and started dating them even though we were two years younger. We thought this made us the two coolest kids around. We both had our first kisses with the girls and were on cloud nine that day.

Eventually, the girls broke up with us. They said Conor's older brother told the entire school that they were dating 5th graders, and they started to get teased by their classmates. We were disappointed, but were happy that we could boast that we were the first boys in our grade to hook up with older girls.

That summer would be my last summer living at The Knolls. The board of directors were trying to put a stop to all of our sports and activities. A few of the families, including ours, were fined by the board for keeping bicycles under the decks and front porches. That was just the beginning. I came home from school one day and was walking off the bus with my brothers and a few friends when we were met with a devastating sight. The Knolls board hired a landscaping company to plant trees in strategic spots to prevent us from playing sports on the fields. In my backyard, they planted a tree right where we put home plate for baseball games, and three more trees were planted in the outfield. At our other field, landscapers planted a tree between first and second base, and another where we would build our jumps for snow tubing in the winter. They even started to call the cops for noise complaints during Manhunt. Sacrilege!

I was furious, so I found the biggest kid in The Knolls, Sean, and had him try to rip the trees out of the ground. When we weren't able to pull the trees out, we cut them at the roots with a large knife. The next day, we were back out on the fields playing. Kids 1, Board of Directors 0.

When we were in 6th grade, the Suffern Hockey parents decided it was time for their kids to start playing travel hockey. Many believe that the only way to really progress quickly was to play travel hockey. There weren't actual practice sessions in a house league, and we only played one game a week. We went to clinics that were offered once a week at the nearby Sport-O-Rama Ice Rink. We participated in drills including power skating, stickhandling, and shooting. Because I have a September birthday, and the cutoff month was July, I was in a league lower than the rest of my friends; the same held true with my status in the Suffern Little League.

The travel team in our area was called the Ramapo Saints. They also played out of the same ice rink as Suffern Hockey. Switching from house league hockey to travel hockey made me extremely nervous. I never tried out for a team before because anyone could participate in a house league, so tryouts were unnecessary. The Saints had three levels which included Double A, A, and B. Double A was the most competitive and players were not guaranteed to make a team. Once the Double A coaches picked their team, there was another tryout for the A team. Once the A team was picked, you had one more shot at making the B team. If you did not make the B team, then your only choice was to try out for a different travel team or play house league. All of my friends who were playing in the Peewee league made one of the three teams. No one made Double A, a few made A, and the rest made B. Since I was in the same grade as my friends, but playing in the Squirt league, a league below Peewee, I was hoping to make the Double A team.

When the first tryout ends, everyone takes off their equipment, puts their street clothes on, and eagerly waits in the lobby for the Double A coach to come out and post the roster. When it came out, I was not on the list. I was disappointed, but thought I could dominate the A team. That wasn't the case either. The A roster came out, and again my name was nowhere to be found. Now I was pissed.

I knew I was better than everyone on that team. What I now know is that there were some serious politics involved on the Ramapo Saints. Most of the kids had been playing travel hockey with the Saints since first or second grade. I was a newcomer, someone who could possibly take the spot of a player who had been playing for years. There were barely any players left at the last tryout for the B team. I still worked really hard even though half the kids could barely skate. The coach came out with the roster, and I could not believe it when my name was not on it. I was devastated. I cried all night, and decided I was going to quit hockey.

All of my Suffern Hockey friends were playing in a league above me and they all managed to make a team. There was no way that I was going to play house league by myself. I never could have guessed that getting cut from the Squirt B team with the Ramapo Saints was the best thing that could have ever happened to me.

One of our Suffern Hockey family friends, the Gabers, told us about a few of their friends who left the Ramapo Saints to play for a newly formed travel team, the Clarkstown Capitals. My parents asked me if I wanted to try out for the team, but I was so upset about getting cut that I just wanted to quit. I only had a few days to make up my mind before the Capitals picked their team. Since they were a new team, there was only one tier at the Squirt B league level.

After a day of moping, my parents convinced me to try out for the Capitals. I was uncomfortable for two reasons: One, I had just got cut from the Ramapo Saints and did not want to have to go through that again, and two, I did not know anyone who was trying out for the Squirt B Clarkstown Capitals. I knew a few guys at the Peewee level who were close friends with the Gabers, but I was too young to play in that league.

I walked into the locker room and it seemed as if most of the kids already knew each other. I sat in the corner and put my equipment on without talking to anyone. Two of the coaches came over and introduced themselves. Coach Rich Willows and Coach Mickey Carroll both had sons on the team, Rich Junior and Mickey Junior.

We took the ice, and I quickly got to work. My father got me fired up, and it was one of the first times I ever heard him curse. "Kick some fucking ass out there!" he shouted. I did exactly that. Both coaches called me and my father over after the first tryout to tell me that I made the team. I was thrilled. I noticed that the kids on this team were very talented, similar to the Double A Squirts with the Ramapo Saints. We were playing in a B league. I knew we were going to dominate, and we did just that.

My experience in 6th grade with the Clarkstown Capitals was the best season I ever had in my entire hockey career. I made many new friends, learned so much about hockey, increased my talent, and was the leading scorer on the team. Best of all, the team had a winning season. We ran through the Squirt B league with ease. I asked the coaches to schedule a game against the Ramapo Saints Squirt B team, but their coach declined to play us because they knew we would destroy them. Coach Mickey Carroll taught me the surf move that year. This involved sprinting full speed down the ice with the puck, taking it wide, and using your body to block the puck from the defenseman, surfing right around him. I scored a lot of goals that season using the surf move. We placed first in our league, and won several tournaments. I was in the best shape of my life. I was training for the Suffern Cross Country Run in the winter of 1999 during gym class at Viola Elementary School. Although I wasn't the fastest sprinter in the school, no one could keep up with me when it came to running long distance due to my endurance training with the Clarkstown Capitals.

We ended up making the playoffs, but lost after a few games. The team split up after that one season, but I played with a few of the guys on different teams throughout my career. The friends I made that season would come to help me immensely my senior year of high school. Things sometimes really do happen for a reason.

In January of 1999, we moved out of our condo in the Knolls and into a house in the Montebello Pines. Our new house was still in Suffern, only about a five-minute drive from the Knolls. The Reimers also lived in the Knolls and moved out at the same time just three houses down from us. It was great having them live so close. Just a few months earlier, Colin's family moved across the street from us.

Like me, Colin also comes from a big family. We did more carpooling with Colin's family than we did with every other family member or friend combined. Whether it was school, practices, games, camps, CCD religion, sleepovers, or birthday parties, it was likely that we would be traveling together.

Even though the Montebello Pines was not in the same zoned area as Viola Elementary, they let Colin and me stay there for the rest of 6th grade. I graduated from Viola Elementary School in June of 1999. Suffern Middle School only included grades 7 and 8 back then.

The summer before 7th grade was a tough time for me. Conor started hanging out more often with his all-star baseball teammates. By the time middle school started, we were no longer friends. It was very strange to not even say hello to him when we passed each other in the hallway. Some of the kids he was hanging out with hacked into my AOL profile and wrote some pretty cruel things. I took it pretty hard at first, but I was lucky to have so many other friends. There are plenty of middle school kids who are less fortunate and lose their only friends, ending up alone.

Mike was not left alone, but he had a similar situation happen to him in middle school. His best friend completely cut him off one day. Worse still, his former best friend had an older kid bully and pick on Mike. When we were in middle school, there were no any anti-bullying movements. On the flipside, AOL instant messenger was the only source of social media that we had.

Facebook, Twitter, Instagram, and Snapchat have changed everything. Cyberbullying is all too real. One post can go viral in a matter of minutes and ruin lives. Middle school is a very tough time for many kids and parents, even more so today with social media. Students have access to information in ways that didn't exist years ago, and this adds yet another layer of stress to their young lives.

I have had some serious in-depth and heartfelt conversations with middle school students after my *Speak Sobriety* presentations. I will never forget the time a middle school student asked a question during the Q&A part of my program. "What does it mean to be sober?" he asked. The entire auditorium started laughing at him. I quickly raised my voice and shut them down, but I could see that he was doing his best to hold back tears. I went over to him and gave him a fist bump, and then made it clear that his question should not have been laughed at and that it was actually a great question. After the assembly, the principal and school social worker thanked me for sticking up for him. They told me that he got picked on all the time.

His question was relevant because I have friends who think they are sober because they don't use heroin or painkillers anymore even though they still drink and smoke marijuana. I have one friend in particular who tells me, "At least I'm sober man," but he drinks alcohol, smokes marijuana, and abuses Xanax. That is not sober; that is denial.

To be sober means to be free from all mind altering substances. There are plenty of people who are sober, but still live a dirty lifestyle. These people are almost certainly doomed, likely to relapse sooner than later. Today, I am clean and sober. That means I live my life by certain principles while being completely free of all mind-altering substances.

CHAPTER 5
The Basement Wrestling Federation (BWF)

Some of my friends, and all of my brothers, loved the World Wrestling Federation (WWF) when we were kids. They had to change the name to World Wrestling Entertainment (WWE) due to a lawsuit brought by the World Wildlife Fund. Much to my surprise, the Panda Bear defeated Hulk Hogan.

We never missed Monday Night Raw or Smackdown. Once a month, the WWE would have a pay per view event which we begged our father to purchase from our cable company. We would order pizza and invite a bunch of friends over to watch. Hulk Hogan, Stone Cold Steve Austin, Bret Hart, Shawn Michaels, and the Undertaker were just a few of our favorites.

We had a huge unfinished basement in our new house. I saw a myriad of opportunities for sports and activities there. Since there was no carpet, we started off with roller hockey. Then, I decided to construct a mini soccer arena. We lived in a new development and there were houses being built everywhere. There was an endless supply of wood that we often "borrowed." I would go to these houses at night and take any scrap wood I could find and bring it back to my house. Some of the pieces may have been a stretch for scrap wood, but we really needed them.

I got bored of basement soccer pretty quickly, and thought of an idea that would turn my basement into a WWE main event. One day after school, I went downstairs and started to build my own wrestling ring. We had a few old mattresses that were used in constructing the basement soccer arena that I laid down to serve as the mat. I then took bungee cords and wrapped them around the poles holding up the house. I set up chairs for a crowd to watch and a table for a cameraman to sit. I used the wood to create an entrance ramp. I gathered a few of my friends and we started BWF, the Basement Wrestling Federation.

How nobody got seriously injured in BWF is nothing short of a miracle. My parents knew we were wrestling, but had no idea how far it went. Of course, I was the craziest of all the wrestlers. I did flips off a chair and a ladder and was willing to take headshots with garbage cans and cookie trays during hardcore matches. I even managed to convince one of my friends to powerbomb me through a wooden table of my own creation. That means he lifted me up over his head and slammed me through the table. BWF lasted until we left middle school. We had 9 events throughout that time and each one was better than the one before.

Conor and his baseball friends tried to copy us and started TWL, the Trampoline Wrestling League. It was a joke. It could not compare to BWF on any level. I ended up inviting Conor to our last event for BWF. He came that night, and we had a long talk. We rekindled our friendship that night and have been best friends ever since. He is one of two friends who have stood by me through my worst years. Ryan Berman is the other. My struggles included experiences that no friends should have to witness.

We videotaped every BWF event, and I decided to make a "Best Of" BWF tape my freshman year of high school. It's fairly easy to make a "Best Of" tape or highlight reel today, but we really didn't have that type of technology in 2001. It was one of those things I don't think I could ever duplicate.

I went through every single tape we had and wrote down the times of the scenes I wanted to use. Then I hooked the camcorder up to a television. That same TV also had a VCR attached. I would play the scene I wanted on the camcorder and press record on the VCR at the same time. I had no idea if this would work, but it did.

I even took it a step further because I wanted background music at the end. I hooked up a PlayStation 2 to the TV instead of the camcorder. I was able to play music on the PlayStation 2 and then press record on the VCR. This miraculously worked too. A few years later, I converted the tape onto a DVD and recently downloaded it to a computer. I gave copies to all of my friends who were a part of BWF. I watch it every few years and can't believe some of the dangerous things that I did.

Speaking of fighting, there was something else going on in Suffern that even outdid the Basement Wrestling Federation. The craziest part was that it was sanctioned by the school. Suffern High School used to host self-defense tournaments for girls. One of the gym teachers taught the girls self-defense moves in gym class. Towards the end of the year, the girls had the option to sign up for the self-defense tournament.

Girls were split up into different weight classes and put into brackets. There was a wrestling mat placed in the center of the gym where the girls would fight. They weren't allowed to throw any punches or kicks and could only use the self-defense moves. Some of the moves these girls used on each other were insane.

The tournament went on all day during school hours. Students were only supposed to go to watch if they had gym class that period or if their teacher brought the whole class down. The first fight I saw lasted for less than 10 seconds. One girl ran at the other full speed, jumped on her, wrapped her legs around her and squeezed until she tapped out. Some of the fights got really aggressive, especially when there were a lot of students cheering the girls on.

Most people who did not attend Suffern High School do not believe me when I tell them about our self-defense tournaments. For a young male high school kid, it was the greatest thing ever. Boys brought cash to school and bet on the girls. One of the craziest moments of high school for me was watching a senior girl power bomb another girl she was fighting in the championship. When she was disqualified, she went nuts and started screaming at the judge/referee telling him it was a legal move. It was the last period of the day so just about the entire school was in the gym screaming.

The administrators eventually banned students from watching, and then got rid of the tournament altogether after a girl suffered a compound fracture of her femur. She sued the Suffern School District and they reached a settlement. Coincidentally, my dad was one of the jurors on the case.

CHAPTER 6
First Blood

When I was a student at Suffern Middle School, I made the junior varsity lacrosse team as an 8th grader. My elementary school gym teacher, Mr. Drab, was the head coach of the team. He also brought a few other 8th graders to the JV squad.

Since we were middle school kids playing a high school sport, we had to pass a physical fitness test in order to be eligible to play. This involved running, a standing long jump, push ups, and sit ups. Luckily, we all passed.

I already knew several people on the team from playing in the early morning lacrosse league at Viola. I was nervous about playing a level up. Most of the other 8th graders playing with me already hit puberty; I did not. I remember being one of the only kids on the team who didn't have any hair on his legs.

I knew I wasn't going to play much; I was just happy to be on the team. One of the best players on the team, Dan, was a sophomore in high school. He did not go to Viola, but he played on a travel team as a youngster. I will never forget the away game bus ride when I first heard him and a few of the other older kids on the team talking about smoking and drinking at a party they attended.

At first, I wasn't able to follow along with everything they were saying. Dan was using phrases like, "I was blazed out of my skull." I heard him ask a few of the other guys if they wanted to "get up on an L later." That meant smoke a blunt. A few of the athletes on the team carried Visine with them. They used it after they smoked weed to eliminate the redness in their eyes. Dan always had a spray canister of Ozium in the glove compartment of his purple Jeep 4Runner. He used that to hide the smell of weed.

By the end of the season, I got better at lacrosse and learned a lot about drugs and alcohol, but not in a good way. No one on the team ever offered me any drugs or alcohol while I was in middle school. Just about every high school player on the junior varsity lacrosse team that year was already drinking alcohol, and a few of them were smoking marijuana.

It wasn't until I got in high school that I first started using drugs and alcohol. Unfortunately, my exposure early on and my need to fit in, be cool, and be accepted by the older kids caused me to seek parties early on in high school.

I had the honor of going back to Suffern Middle School recently to speak to the 8th grade students. The current principal, Mr. Fox, remembered me from when he was an assistant principal at Suffern High School and I was a student. He was very supportive in bringing me to the school to share my story with the students.

I ran into one of my high school science teachers, Mr. Sullivan, when I went back to Suffern Middle School to give my *Speak Sobriety* presentation. Mr. Sullivan also worked at Suffern High School when I was a student there. After a few minutes of catching up, he asked if I thought playing up with older kids on the junior varsity lacrosse team as an 8th grader influenced my getting involved with drugs and alcohol at such an early age. I never thought about that aspect of my addiction before, but upon reflection, I believe it did.

Transition phases are some of the most crucial times in life, especially for young students. The transition from middle school to high school, and then high school to college can be overwhelming.

Students who are not ready for the peer pressure and temptations that come with high school can find themselves in trouble quickly. I was one of those students who was only concerned with being cool and hanging out with older kids who were partying. Bad decisions at various stages often come with serious consequences. In my case, my transition from middle school to high school was bad, and high school to college was disastrous.

I was in Mr. Sullivan's class my senior year of high school. He was one of my teachers who really gave me a chance and never judged me based on my reputation and what other teachers were saying. By the time I was a senior, I was stuck with the label of "the bad kid."

Mr. Sullivan asked me to stay after class my first day of school senior year. Of course, I assumed I was in trouble or about to be blamed for something. To my surprise he just wanted to let me know that he did not care what other students and teachers said about me, and that he would only judge me based on my character and behavior in his classroom. I really appreciated him saying that. I never got in trouble in his class. I didn't get straight A's, but I treated him with respect, just as he treated me.

I did not have the problem of entering high school with a bad reputation since I had not developed one as a middle school student. The worst thing I did in middle school was start a food fight. Our cafeteria was under construction and since our school had two gyms, the administrators decided to turn one of them into a cafeteria. The food fight was planned all week. It was the end of the school year, and we planned the fight for that Friday. I do not know how we managed to keep it a secret from the faculty for an entire week.

I coordinated with my friend, Yan, who sat on the other side of the gym (cafeteria). He threw a sandwich across the gym at my friend's table. Yan sat under the basketball hoop, so I proceeded to shake up a soda can and toss it across the gym and it exploded against the backboard. A student with long, spiked hair stood up and screamed, "FOOD FIGHT"!

The food fight lasted about 30 seconds, but it seemed like forever. The lunch monitors ran out of the room because students were purposely throwing food at them. It was insane. My friends and I still talk about that day. Students were asked to write down names of those who began the fight. Yan and I were called to the principal's office on Monday morning. We were told our names were repeatedly mentioned. A few other kids who sat at our tables ended up on the list as well. We all denied starting it and ended up having to stay after school for a week to help the janitors sweep and clean.

After I spoke to a small group of middle school students at the Wyckoff YMCA in May of 2017, one of the supervisors came up to me and thanked me for speaking. He said he taught at a high school for many years and it always bothered him when teachers made negative comments about students. He believes that puts teachers in the mindset before the first day of class that a particular student is trouble and should be dealt with accordingly.

Soon enough, middle school graduation came and I was off for the summer in anticipation of starting high school in the fall. That summer, I went to a hockey camp in Toronto with my Suffern Hockey friends, Colin and Jason. I played in a few summer lacrosse and hockey leagues, but mostly just hung out with my friends and played pickup sports. This would be my last summer of innocence. Over the next year, I became a completely different person, a Jekyll and Hyde, except I was mostly Hyde. Under the influence of drugs and alcohol as a 14-year-old, my brain was a veritable sponge for negativity and bad behaviors, and I soaked up every last bit. The sponge was never wrung out; I was strung out.

CHAPTER 7
Pep Rally

I remember my first day of high school vividly. I boarded the bus with Mike and neighbors, Colin and Brendan. Colin and I were freshmen, Mike was a sophomore, and Brendan was a junior. Mike and Brendan were telling us about the different groups in school. The jocks, preps, skaters, nerds, and the *ghetto* kids. Brendan told Colin and me that we would be hard to identify because we dressed like skaters one day, wearing Independence clothing, and then Abercrombie & Fitch the next. Brendan said we needed to pick a side. The summer before high school, Colin and I became immersed in skateboarding. That faded out, and we were seen as just another pair of preppy jocks.

Although there were many different groups and cliques in high school, there were three activities that brought everyone together. Drugs, alcohol, and parties. One Friday, the seniors threw a huge party at the end of Westgate Road by the back entrance to Kakiat Park. My friend, Rob, lived just a few houses down from where the party was taking place. I was with about ten of my friends when we decided to walk to the party. Many of us had older siblings who were already there.

I felt excitedly nervous as we rolled up to the party together. When we got to the end of the street, I could not believe my eyes. There were hundreds of Suffern High School students drinking and smoking in the middle of the street. There were multiple kegs of beer hidden in the woods by the back entrance to the park and a few of the seniors were selling red solo cups for $5 each. Some of my friends were too scared to buy a cup; most of us were not, and of course, I was one of the bold ones.

One of my older friends came over and took me under his wing. He brought me over to the keg where a few guys were sitting around holding court. One of them asked me, "First time?" I answered, "Yes," and the upperclassmen proceeded to pump the tap and pour me my first beer. I felt like the coolest kid in the world as I took a big gulp of Bud Light. Everywhere I looked I was seeing orange dots getting brighter and then dimmer repeatedly. The dots were the ends of the cigarettes and blunts being smoked. I was offered a cigarette by one of my older friends, a lacrosse player. He lit it for me, and as I took my first puff, I immediately started coughing, but I loved the feeling.

My hockey teammate walked me around the party through clouds of smoke with a red solo cup in one hand and a cigarette in the other. I was introduced to some of his friends and older girls. One of the girls at the party was a senior; her name was Emily. Just like most of the other students at the party, Emily was a good kid. She was very pretty and a popular scholar-athlete. I did not know her personally, but some of my friends were close to her.

I barely made it through one weekend as a high school student without drinking alcohol and smoking cigarettes. I arrived at school Monday morning, walking the halls with a bit more confidence and swagger. I was getting dapped up by some of my older friends as a congratulations for drinking and smoking. A few of my friends had already drank and smoked before that night, but it was the first time for most of us. The next day was Tuesday, September 11, 2001. Partying stood in sharp contrast to the tragedy that we experienced on that fateful day.

I was sitting in Mrs. Buchanan's Earth Science class with a bunch of my friends that morning. I hated science, but loved the class because most of my friends were with me. Conor was in the class as well. Another teacher came running into the classroom and called Mrs. Buchanan into the hallway. After a few seconds, we heard Mrs. Buchanan scream. She came back in and told us to be quiet and wait for an announcement. I had no idea what was about to transpire. A few minutes later, the principal came on the loudspeaker and informed us that one of the Twin Towers at the World Trade Center was hit by a plane. Initially, I didn't think it was anything too crazy. I had no idea it was a terrorist attack and how that plane crash would forever change the lives of innocent Americans.

When the first plane hit, I assumed it was an accident, as did many others. Then the second plane hit. This is when things started to get out of control in school. Students were panicking and in shock. Parents were ringing the main office phones and calling their children's cell phones. America was under attack. More reports started coming in with each passing minute. The first tower collapsed, then the second.

I had no idea about Al Qaeda or who Osama Bin Laden was until that day. It was made clear that the plane crash was no accident once the second plane hit the second tower. Al Qaeda took credit for the attack, and it was officially an act of war against America.

I got off the bus at a friend's house that day and stopped at a local deli. Everyone was being more polite than usual. My friends and I were all feeling patriotic that day and even talked about joining the military once we were old enough.

It took a few weeks for things to get back to normal, but then tragedy struck the members of Suffern High School personally. Every school year in October, the school hosted a pep rally. Each class was given a color to represent. Freshmen wore purple, sophomores red, juniors green, and seniors wore blue. The school made t-shirts for each class and students painted their faces in a wide array of designs. Some of the girls added glitter and other accessories to their school-spirited ensembles.

We all piled into the gym and were split up into our respective classes. The band played songs, the cheerleaders cheered, and the rest of the students rallied with pride.

Hazing was a big part of the pep rally. The seniors would capture freshman and tie them up. Two of my close friends were duct taped together, put into a garbage can, and rolled out into the middle of the gym in front of the entire school. The teachers and faculty turned a blind eye to the hazing and allowed it to happen as long as no one was physically injured. Being hazed as a freshman was basically a rite of passage.

The pep rally ended at lunch time, and many seniors piled into their cars and left for the day. But there was something going on that day that the school administration was not aware of. Some of the students, especially the upperclassmen, were drunk. A few girls in particular drank before school the morning of the pep rally. They also brought in water bottles filled with vodka and were drinking throughout the day. Three girls left in a convertible at lunch time. Emily, the girl at the party a few weeks earlier, was one of the passengers in the back seat of the convertible.

A former Suffern High School student was driving behind the girls and witnessed the tragedy that occurred soon after the girls left the school. He said that the three girls were singing and dancing when the driver lost control of the car. The convertible flipped over, landing on top of Emily. The paramedics came quickly and did everything they could, but Emily didn't make it. She died that afternoon at Good Samaritan Hospital, just a few minutes from the school.

The next day left the school community in shock. Students and faculty alike were crying uncontrollably while hugging and consoling each other. The principal addressed the students on the loudspeaker in an effort to bring us together. There was a long moment of silence for Emily. Close friends gathered together at the crash site after school and laid down flowers. Although I did not know Emily on a personal level, she was the first person my age that I ever heard of dying as a result of substance use. Sadly, the young man who witnessed the accident recently died of a heroin overdose. This is an evil, invisible enemy that destroys lives and is blind to age or innocence.

Emily's death got a lot of attention and media coverage. There are many sensitive issues in this book, and I don't always use real names, but Emily's story is public knowledge and still talked about today. Parents, teachers, and police started communicating. Emily's parents helped create The Ramapo Rescuing Our Youth coalition in an effort to raise awareness about the dangers of substance use and abuse. Programs from Mothers Against Drunk Driving (M.A.D.D.) were implemented at our school. Some students close with Emily talked about staying sober in her honor. It's sad to say that the shock of Emily's death only lasted for a short time. Before long, many students went back to their old ways. Some never stopped partying at all.

Suffern High School has made many changes since the 2001 pep rally. The present administration takes every precaution necessary to ensure student safety.

I bring up the tragedy of Emily at my presentations because she was a typical student who lost her life because of one bad decision. After some of my presentations, some students have told me that they know they aren't addicts. Even if that is true, Emily was not an addict or an alcoholic either. You do not have to be addicted to drugs and alcohol for bad things to happen. Emily made one bad decision, and she lost her life because of it. Moreover, just because a student makes it through high school or even college without the serious negative consequences that can come from substance use, that does not mean it cannot happen soon after college, or later on in life.

This is especially true today with the prescription drug and heroin epidemic. Most people I know who ended up addicted to opioids such as OxyContin, heroin, or both, started out in their early to mid twenties. Much of this was due to the timing of the drug epidemic in America.

I only drank alcohol twice the first semester of my freshman year of high school, and it was never more than a beer or two. I was doing well in school and getting ready to try out for the varsity ice hockey team. Suffern Hockey was the most well-known sport in the school. We were always the best team in Section 1, which consisted of Rockland and Westchester County.

I dreamed of playing on the Suffern varsity ice hockey team since I was in elementary school. We all went to games on Friday nights to watch the team play. The up and coming Suffern hockey players would wear their jerseys to the varsity games, which got us free admission. The stands were always packed with diehard fans. The student section at the end was loud and rowdy. At the time, I was unaware that many students would drink before the games. I know that when I was on the team, at least half of the people in the student section showed up with a nice buzz at the start of each game.

My freshman year was a unique one for Suffern Hockey. The team had just graduated ten seniors. It would have been eleven but the star player left after his junior year to play in the USHL in the Midwest. He ended up playing Division One college hockey for Denver and won two national championships.

The senior class coming up only had one player, the junior class had a few, and the sophomore class had three. This gave the freshman class an opportunity to make the team and even get some ice time. Nine freshmen and one 8th grader replaced the ten seniors that graduated the year before. My friends and I were so excited to make the team and immediately ordered our varsity jackets. It meant something when you walked around Suffern High School wearing the varsity hockey jacket. It was a symbol of accomplishment and respect.

My three best friends on the team were Colin, Jesse, and David. We did everything together that year. Colin and I built a mini hockey arena in my basement and we played two on two games almost every weekend. One of my younger brothers would set up a video camera and tape our games.

I didn't drink or smoke once during my entire freshman hockey season. I was taking my role as an athlete seriously because I was getting playing time. The team wasn't as good as it was in the past because we barely had any upperclassmen. We still won the section, but got killed in the state quarterfinals by West Genesee in upstate New York. The hockey season ended and there was a short reprieve before lacrosse season began. That first weekend after the hockey season ended, I made a decision that would change my life forever. It was the beginning of my nightmare.

CHAPTER 8
The Gateway to Hell

Every day after school I was taking the bus with my hockey friends to the Sport-O-Rama Ice Rink for practice. Now that the season was over, I had about a week with nothing to do before lacrosse season started. I got a ride home from one of my friends, a senior, who I grew up with in The Knolls. There were two other seniors in the car with him. As soon as they pulled out of the school parking lot, they all lit up cigarettes. I was offered one, and of course I accepted.

Then the driver asked me if I ever blazed (smoked pot). I said no, but that I wanted to try it. He told me that he could get it for me anytime I wanted and to just give him a call if I wanted to give it a try. He dropped me off at my house, and I thought about that for the rest of the day. I talked about it with two of my friends in school the next day. They had already tried smoking weed, and were down to do it again.

The next day I went up to my friend and told him I wanted to buy a bag of weed. He said if I gave him $20 he would bring it to me after school. I had the $20 on me, so I reached into my pocket and gave it to him. He smiled and nodded at me, then walked away.

Sure enough, I got the call less than an hour after school to meet him on the corner of my street. I got on my dirt bike and pretended to go ride in the trails down the street. He came around the corner quickly, and I went up to his car window and he handed me a small bag of weed inside a Ziploc bag. There was a small glass object in the bag as well. He told me there was a little extra present inside, then said, "enjoy" and drove away.

The extra present was a glass bowl that I could use to smoke the weed.

I got home and called my friends and told them we were good to go for Friday night. I held onto my contraband for a few days, hiding it behind a picture frame in my room. Once the sun set on Friday night, my friends and I walked down my street to find a place to light up. We decided to go into a house on my street that was still under construction. The three of us walked inside and I took out the bag.

One of my friends had smoked a few times, so he knew what to do. He took a small chunk out of the bag and broke it up into little pieces, packing it into the end of the glass bowl. He then handed me the bowl and said, "It's your first time; you do the honors." He lit the bowl for me as I inhaled. I tried to hold it in, but immediately started coughing. My friends laughed and I did too. We took turns passing around the bowl, taking one hit after another.

Once we finished, we walked around my development for a few hours because we were scared to go back to my house. We didn't want our parents to find out that we were stoned. I brought Visine and a bottle of Curve cologne with me to get rid of my red eyes and mask the smell of smoke. I learned that trick on the junior varsity lacrosse team in 8th grade.

My friends were laughing and repeatedly stated how stoned they were. I said I was too, but I wasn't really sure. It wasn't the feeling I was expecting. After a few hours of walking around, we went back to my house, ate a bunch of junk food, and went to sleep.

The next morning, my parents went away for the entire day, so Mike and I decided to have a few friends over. I knew a few of my brother's friends smoked every now and then, so I told them I had smoked for the first time the night before. One of them reached into his pocket and pulled out a bigger bag of weed and an even bigger glass bowl than the night before. He said, "I'll get you up on this, you get me back next time." I watched him as he took a big hit. He held it in for a while, and exhaled slowly. Then he passed the bowl to me. I took a hit, then blew out the smoke. He laughed and said, "You're not inhaling; you won't get high unless you do." I told him that I didn't really feel that different last night after I smoked. He told me that after I suck the smoke into my mouth, I had to then inhale it into my lungs. "You are going to cough like crazy at first, but you will get used to it."

I took another hit, but this time I inhaled the smoke into my lungs. Sure enough, I started coughing immediately. It was painful to inhale into virgin lungs, but I felt the effects instantly. I kept on smoking, but had to drop out after my third hit. I was wasted and went inside and laid on the couch. It was a scary yet exciting feeling for me to be truly high for my first time.

Smoking pot became a weekend habit from that day forward. I drank alcohol when there were house parties, but smoked almost every weekend. I managed to still get good grades and was the leading scorer on the junior varsity lacrosse team my freshman year. My parents had not caught on during my freshman year, mostly because there weren't any negative consequences as a result of my drug use: at least not yet. Freshman year ended with a huge party at my friend's house. He had an older sister who was going into her senior year of high school. There were a lot of people at the party, including my friend Dan, who I met on the JV lacrosse team as an 8th grader. That night, he called me over and made me an offer I could not refuse.

CHAPTER 9
Deal or No Deal: DEAL

The first summer party of 2002 was outdoors in an enormous backyard. It was a big piece of property with more than enough room to fit everyone. Dan brought me to the back corner of the backyard so no one else could see us. He reached into his pocket, and handed me 14 individual dime bags inside a Ziploc bag. He said, "This is a half-ounce of weed. I want you to sell it to all of your friends or anyone else who wants to smoke. Sell each bag for $20 and you will make back $280. Give me $200, and keep the $80 profit for yourself."

I didn't even have to think about his offer. I put the half-ounce into the pocket of my cargo shorts and started spreading the word that I was "holding," which meant I had weed for sale. Dan also spread the word to some of the upperclassmen. Just a few minutes went by and I had my first sale. It was one of my older brother's friends. He bought two bags for $40. Then another person bought a bag, and another. Within a few hours, the half-ounce was gone. I didn't even get a chance to smoke one. I went over to Dan who was smoking in the corner with a few of his friends and handed him the $200. He was shocked. He couldn't believe I sold it all in just a few hours. The blunt they were smoking came around to Dan, he said "No, give it to Steve, he deserves it." I grabbed the blunt and took two big hits, then passed it down.

I wasn't sure whether or not this was going to be just a one time thing. A few minutes later an older kid, who had already graduated from high school and was a well-known drug dealer, came to the party. I watched him and Dan walk out to the street and get into a car. A few minutes later, they returned to the party. Dan came up to me and said, "We need to talk." We walked down the street where Dan's car was parked. I got into the passenger seat and from under his shirt, Dan pulled out a quarter pound of weed.

I never saw so much weed in my life. He had a digital scale in his center console and took it out as our business partnership began. We started weighing out individual grams for me to sell. He handed me another 14 bags, and said, "We are going to make a lot of money and smoke for free."

We went back to the house party and into the basement. Another friend of mine, Brendan, was about to start rolling a blunt. He asked me if I had ever rolled one before. I said that I had smoked blunts, but never rolled one. He was more than happy to teach me and pulled out a second cigar out of his 4-pack of Dutch Masters. I rolled my own blunt as I watched Brendan roll his. He licked the outside of the cigar to get the paper moist and then began unraveling it. He laid the paper out on a table, and I did the same. Then he split the cigar down the middle, and emptied the tobacco into the trash. Next, he filled up the inner layer of the cigar with weed and proceeded to roll it up. He lined up the rolled up cigar on an angle at the end of the outer layer, wrapping it up into a blunt. Mine didn't come out nearly as good, but it was smokable. We went outside and smoked our own blunts and called it smoking one to the dome.

A girl, who was a classmate of mine, came over to me and asked if she could get a few hits and I gladly obliged. We started taking hits and exhaling the smoke into each other's mouths, we called it shottis. I ended up making out with her that night. I felt like I was the king of the world at that party. Alcohol, drugs, money, and girls. What more could I want? I wished that night would never end. In hindsight, I wish it never began.

Dan drove Brendan and me home at 2:30 in the morning. Our friend Ben was with us too, and we smoked one last time in the car at the bottom of my driveway. I walked inside just after 3a.m. This was the latest I had ever stayed out. I told my parents I was sleeping at my friend Rob's house since he was throwing the party. They weren't expecting me to come home. Mike was at the same party with his friends, but they left a few hours before I did. I was always the last one to leave the party. I never wanted it to end...and that was just the beginning.

My description of what transpired at the first party of the summer of 2002 sounds as if I am glorifying the use of drugs and alcohol at high school parties. For me, on that night, I was in my glory days. I wasn't a hardcore drug addict living on the streets and committing heinous crimes to support my habit. I was a 14-year-old middle to upper class white kid enjoying the summer and looking forward to his sophomore year of high school. I had not experienced any negative consequences as a result of my drug and alcohol use. There is a saying that I have heard in the recovery community: "My worst day sober is better than my best day high." I don't know who came up with that saying, but it's ridiculous.

People don't start out using drugs and alcohol because they make them feel bad. They do it because it makes them feel good. I have heard substance abuse presentations where an older person will get up and try to scare the students straight. That approach has been proven to be ineffective. Students take me seriously and listen to my presentation because I am completely open and honest. I concede to some of their arguments. The issues surrounding underage drinking and drug use are not black and white. If they were, Americans wouldn't be in the middle of a drug epidemic.

Of course, high school parties start out fun. The problem is that fun often comes with risks, and the good times don't last for everyone. They certainly did not last for me. The good times were becoming few and far between, and before I realized it, I was a full-blown drug addict and a criminal. My lifestyle was completely mindless. There were no more parties for me to attend. Nobody wanted me around. That summer was the beginning of a decade-long descent towards self-destruction.

I am often asked during the Q&A portion of my program: "Do you blame your friend that got you started dealing drugs?" My answer is an emphatic, "No!" Of course, I don't blame him. Dan wasn't even the first person who sold me drugs. In fact, I am happy to report that Dan has been clean and sober longer than I have. He volunteers his time and does service work for those who are still suffering. He has helped countless people in their recovery, including me. He is a true friend and I am grateful to have him in my life.

The blame game for addiction doesn't work, especially when you get started as a teenager. I was introduced to drugs by an older kid, and then I introduced other kids to drugs in the same way. It's a domino effect that has no end. My goal is to stop the drug domino effect and start a new one for sobriety and healthy choices.

CHAPTER 10
The Beginning of the End

I was a completely different person at the start of my sophomore year of high school. I met up with all the boys from 42 Gang before school to smoke blunts. We weren't an actual gang; we just called ourselves the 42 Gang because that represented 4/20, National Marijuana Smoking Day. Most of the kids in 42 Gang were seniors, including Dan. There was one junior, and I was the only sophomore. My initiation into 42 Gang was to break a car window and steal an ashtray from a Honda Civic. One of the seniors had lost his ashtray and used my initiation as a way of getting another one. I wanted to be part of the crew so badly, although hesitant at first, I gave into the peer pressure. They soon found the car they were looking for in a parking lot, and I did the rest.

I walked into my first day of school as a sophomore under the influence of marijuana. I was as high as a kite, but used the standard tricks to cover it up. I put Visine in my eyes, sprayed cologne, washed my hands, and changed my shirt.

I hung out with several different groups of friends my sophomore year of high school. My core group of friends, the older kids from 42 Gang, the Suffern Hockey guys, and Mike's friends.

My core group of friends started to hang out with the freshmen girls during our sophomore year. One of my best friends, Ryan, had a younger sister, Danielle, who was a freshman when we were sophomores. One of Danielle's friends decided she was going to have some people over on a Friday night at the start of the 2002-2003 school year. It was supposed to be just her group of friends and my group of friends, no more than 30

58

people. Word got out, and her little get together turned into an open house party.

Open house parties are crazy enough, but it's even worse when it's at a freshman girl's house whose parents are away. Half the school showed up and her house got trashed. It was a nightmare for her, especially at such a young age. People punched holes in the wall, broke a few doors, and stole jewelry and electronics. I even saw a few seniors steal her dad's golf clubs and start hitting balls over the house while others were hitting balls directly into the house.

I slept at the freshman girl's house that night because I was hooking up with one of her friends. I remember being in the bed with this girl when I heard a car drive by and smash her mailbox. I woke up the next morning to this poor girl screaming and crying. A few of my friends slept over as well. We did what we could to help clean up, but there really wasn't much we could do as the damage was too much to fix.

My behavior had already started to change the previous summer, but now it was carrying over into my academics. I failed my first class my sophomore year. My history teacher and I did not get along well and clashed often. I was ineligible to play for three hockey games because I was failing his class.

The head coach of the varsity hockey team was also my guidance counselor. He was very disappointed in me and could see I was headed for trouble. I thought I was getting back at my history teacher by not paying attention in his class or doing any work, not realizing I was only sabotaging myself.

My teacher and I got into an argument during the fall sports season. He was coaching one of the teams and I was doing off ice training with the hockey team. He heard me curse, and told me to do 50 push ups. I laughed, and cursed again. He doubled it to 100. I cursed again and said, "Let's see how high you can count." I ended up running hills, but only because my hockey coach told me to. A year earlier I would have never said anything like that. If another teacher or coach heard me curse and told me to do 50 push ups, I would have done them immediately. My brain was changing; my thought process was completely different from earlier years. I began to believe that I could do whatever I wanted and felt I was untouchable and immune to any punishment or authority.

Once I was eligible to play hockey, I worked my way up to the first line. I was starting as a sophomore; however, this season was far different from the last. Although every high school team in Rockland and Westchester was in section 1, the majority of them were in Division 2 my freshman year. That meant that we didn't have to play any of those teams at playoff time. My sophomore year, many teams switched to Division 1, which meant we had much tougher competition. The Clarkstown North Rams, from the next town over, were our rivals. I knew most of the players on their team from camps and travel hockey.

Clarkstown North ended up beating us in the section finals 7-1. Their three best players and goalie graduated that year, and we were pumped up for the next season. Colin, David, Jesse and me dreamed about winning a state championship just like the 1992 Suffern Hockey team. We were ready to accomplish that feat in our junior year.

When lacrosse season began in the spring of 2003, there was still snow on the ground. This meant the first few weeks we would be practicing on concrete in the parking lot of Spook Rock Pool, about a mile run from the school.

By this time, I was smoking pot every day, and I could feel the negative effects on my stamina. Oddly, my motivation and athletic drive to play hockey was not affected by drugs and alcohol in the same way that lacrosse was. The effort I put in at lacrosse tryouts my sophomore year was a complete embarrassment. I was one of the last to show up at tryouts on our run from the school. I put in minimal effort on drills and sometimes even stayed at the back of the line so I did not have to participate.

In hindsight, I am still not sure why I acted the way I did. If I did not want to play lacrosse, I could have simply opted out of the tryouts and chosen not to play. But I didn't; I still showed up. The only rationale I can come up with is that somewhere deep down inside of me, I still wanted to compete and play on the team as I did my entire life, but the drugs had taken control of me. Some players on the team were potheads but still practiced and played with maximum effort. I was able to do that in hockey, but not in lacrosse.

I was one of the only players in the sophomore class not to make the varsity team. The coach told me I was the first student to ever make junior varsity as an 8th grader, and still be on the team as a sophomore. He couldn't understand why I went downhill so quickly, and I couldn't either. He said that there was no way he could put me on varsity given my poor performance and lack of initiative. Although he was correct, I wasn't even upset when I did not make it onto the varsity squad.

My parents were so upset when they heard I did not make the varsity lacrosse team.

I wanted to quit, but I would have had to miss a quarter of the next season, which was hockey. That was a school rule that was meant to encourage kids to stick it out and learn how to not become quitters. I believe that was a fair and effective rule, and there was no way I was going to miss 25% of the hockey season, so I stuck it out.

A loophole in that rule is that it isn't written anywhere that you have to give 100% effort. I gave less than 50%. I was the leading scorer on the junior varsity lacrosse team my freshman year and now, a year later, I wasn't even in the starting lineup. I became ineligible to play for a few lacrosse games because I was failing history class again. I couldn't have cared less and I started falling deeper into the abyss; however, I could never have predicted how far I could fall.

At the end of the season, the varsity coach brought up a few junior varsity players to varsity. He called me into his office and told me he was going to bring me up. He said, "You should have been on this team to begin with and should have had a lot of playing time. I'm hoping that bringing you up with your friends will motivate you to get it together for next year."

The team made the playoffs that year. I dressed for the game, but had no shot of ever walking onto the field. We lost in the playoffs, and the season was over. I remember how upset Dan was. He was a senior and it was all over for him. He told me to do things differently next year or I would regret it once my high school career was over.

CHAPTER 11
The Big Leagues

Before the summer of my junior year, I had not tried any other drugs besides marijuana and alcohol. Some of my friends had tried Xanax, which is a Benzodiazepine, sometimes referred to as "the housewife drug". There is a stereotype in the drug culture that Xanax is prescribed to older women who are stressed about nothing. I believe Xanax is over prescribed, yet there are some people with severe anxiety who really need drugs such as Xanax, Klonopin, or Valium. Most of my friends did not fall into that category.

There were a few dealers in Suffern who had large supplies of Xanax; others would get prescriptions or steal them from their parents and sell them on the street. I was taking a medication called Trileptal intermittently for my ADHD my freshman and sophomore year. I was taking it less my sophomore year, and had completely stopped before the end of the school year.

The label on my prescription said not to mix with other drugs or drink with alcohol. I smoked pot and drank while taking the medication, but I was scared to mix other pills with Trileptal. I was no longer taking them, and when the opportunity presented itself, I tried Xanax for my first time and I liked the feeling it gave me.

A few days later, I tried cocaine for the first time with all the guys from 42 Gang. We stayed up all night at one of our friend's houses because his parents were away. We were drinking, smoking, and banging lines of cocaine all night. Then we all took Xanax to help come down off of the cocaine. We repeated this ritual often in the summer of 2003. Some of my core group of friends also started messing around with cocaine that summer, but none of them did it as often as I did.

Just before Mike's senior year and my junior year, we threw a big party at the house. My parents were out so we had the house to ourselves. All of the popular upperclassmen were there, and we also invited freshmen and sophomore girls. The party was outside in the backyard and everyone was having a great time until a group of guys who had graduated two years earlier came to fight two friends of ours who were dating their ex-girlfriends.

It was past midnight and things got out of control fast. People were yelling and screaming at each other, and a fight broke out. Luckily, one of my older friends, a really big guy, was able to shut down the fight pretty quickly. I knew it was a matter of time before the cops showed up. One of my neighbors and a friend of mine started cleaning up as fast as they could. We didn't have a keg that night, so there were beer bottles everywhere. We cleaned up everything in under five minutes. Then my neighbor picked up the two garbage cans over his back and ran deep into the woods behind my house to throw everything away.

Minutes later, the cops showed up, but there was no evidence of any underage drinking at the party. The cops made everyone go home, but no one got in trouble that night. This was just a preview of the crazy parties that would come in my junior year.

CHAPTER 12
Crash

Mike and his friends turned our basement into a really cool hangout spot. It was unfinished, so we didn't have to worry about getting it dirty. We had a pool table, ping pong table, black lights, glow in the dark posters, television, CD player, card table, and a few old couches.

A few of Mike's friends were potheads like me, except they were able to do well in school and live productive lives. Almost every weekend, my basement was the after hours smoking spot.

Whether it was after a house party or a low key night, any of our friends who wanted to smoke and listen to chill music like Phish, Pink Floyd, or The Doors ended up in the basement. Some of them came just to hang out and didn't smoke. Mike would usually just man the CD player and pick the music and act as the resident DJ.

I would make sure my parents were sleeping, then bring everyone quietly into the basement. To cover up the smell of weed, we would make a bag of popcorn and burn it just a little bit, then open it up right at the top of the basement stairs. We took a towel and covered the bottom of the doors, opened the windows, and put on a fan. Luckily, the basement was concrete, so there wasn't anywhere for the smell to be absorbed.

As stated earlier, I have heard the zero tolerance approach at substance abuse presentations often. This is when someone tries to scare students straight by telling them anyone who smokes pot or drinks alcohol before they are of legal age will end up addicted, possibly in jail or even dead.

Simply put, that is not true. All of Mike's friends drank alcohol in high school, some of them smoked pot, and none of them ended up with negative consequences because of their use. The first two parts are the same for my friends as well, but a good amount of us ended up with serious negative consequences due to drug and alcohol use. Some of my friends have lost their lives from an overdose or drunk driving accident. Others ended up in jail or prison with criminal records.

When I share my story with students, I concede that there are some people who can drink alcohol and live productive lives. There are also some individuals who smoke marijuana and live relatively "normal" lives. I concede to this argument because students will tune you out if you start lying to them and talking down to them. You need to validate their reality.

I once heard a guy giving a substance abuse presentation say the following: "If you ever smoke weed or drink alcohol in high school, you are going to end up dead, in jail, or if you are lucky, in rehab." I watched the students roll their eyes at this false statement. Once students hear this, they stop listening and no longer think that the presenter is making honest claims.

Of course, I discuss the dangers of drug and alcohol use and some of the misconceptions, especially about marijuana. My overall approach is different. When I speak to students, I make it clear that I am not there to preach to them, but simply to share my story and engage in a discussion about the issues surrounding substance use and abuse. I always put the onus on the students and let them know the decision is theirs. Of course, there are many people in their lives to assist them, but they have to decide for themselves what they really want to do with their lives, and if taking the risk of ending up with major substance abuse issues as I did is worth it. I am living proof that it isn't.

I never want to send the wrong message that if you have tried drugs or alcohol and don't have a problem now, then you will not in the future. I talk about several friends of mine who made it through high school or even college without any substance abuse issues, but they had major struggles later on. I couldn't even make it through my junior year before things got really bad for me.

My first Friday as a junior was the home opener for our football team. A friend of mine decided to throw a pre-game party. She lived down the street from the middle school where the football team played at night under the lights. We all got hammered drunk and walked over to the game. Everyone was having a great time, but one of my friends was belligerently drunk. I was wasted too, but not as bad as he was. We left the game at halftime and walked back to our friends' house where we initially pre-gamed.

My friend had his car parked at the house where we were partying. We were planning on sitting in his car and listening to Dave Matthews Band and smoking cigarettes until everyone got back from the game. Neither of us were in any condition to drive. After 15 minutes of sitting in his car with the windows down, a few more people showed up at the house. The street was dark so no one saw us in the car.

All of a sudden, my friend started the car, put it in drive, and off we went. At the end of the road, which was only about 30 feet from where we were parked, we had a choice to make a right or a left. My friend drove directly into a tree. We were only going about 15 miles per hour, so we were not hurt. I heard a few friends scream and start running towards the car. Before they could get to us, my friend backed up onto the road and headed home.

What we didn't know was that he knocked out one of his headlights, and there was visible damage to the front end of the car. Both of us were completely wasted, but we somehow made it all the way to his street. When we arrived, we saw a police car; I thought we were doomed. The cop must not have seen the busted headlight or the damage to the front end because he kept on driving. My friend parked the car and we ran into his house. We got lucky that night, but over time, my luck ran out.

CHAPTER 13
The Virgin Islands

A few of my friends lost their virginity at the beginning of the school year. I was waiting for the next big party to have sex with a girl who I was already hooking up with. One of my close friends threw a huge keg party a few weeks into the school year, something he continued once a month on Saturday nights. Some of what went down at these parties is too graphic to recount, but there was a lot of reckless behavior by many.

Once the night was over, we did our usual routine and a few select guys went back to my house to smoke. This time, I had Mike's friend Dave drive the girl I was hooking up with to my house. When everyone else went downstairs to smoke, I went upstairs with her to my bedroom.

We ended up going on my roof first and smoked together. While we were getting high, I got a call from Dave telling me that he was leaving and if the girl needed a ride home, she had to come down now. I told him she didn't need a ride and I would get her one. He knew me pretty well, and called me out on my lie. He said, "I don't want you stealing your mom's car and driving her home high at 3a.m. with only a Learner's Permit." I promised him that would not happen, but he was skeptical.

Then Dave, the only sober ride home that night, left. I finished smoking and went back inside with her. We wasted no time and started making out. One thing led to another, and I ended up losing my virginity that night. Shortly after, I stole my mom's truck and drove her home at 3 a.m., just as Dave predicted. I dropped her off and got home safely. I was so excited I couldn't even sleep that night. I had only recently turned 16 and I wasn't a virgin anymore. I thought things were becoming exciting for me, but this was just the calm before the storm.

CHAPTER 14
Into the Wild

I was really pumped up about the upcoming hockey season. As a junior, I was one of the better players on the team. I was able to maintain passing grades simply to remain eligible to play hockey. Even though I wasn't failing any classes, my behavior off the ice was getting increasingly worse each day. I was using Xanax and cocaine, smoking and selling weed, and staying out late on school nights. More often than not, I was getting into arguments with my parents.

The harder drugs made my life spiral out of control quickly. I became a very angry person. I was punching holes in the wall and had a very short fuse. On the second day of hockey tryouts, I was slashed in the back of the leg multiple times by a freshman. I turned around in anger and broke his stick in half by slashing it with mine.

In my opinion, the school administration and the kid's parents turned this into a much bigger deal than it really was. The year before, I watched one of the captains of our team and another upperclassman fight on the ice without any consequences other than the team having to skate suicides. I believe that was the right way to handle it. This was ice hockey, a contact sport that even allows fighting at the professional level. There are certain situations where the school should intervene, but for the most part, problems between teammates should be left at "boys will be boys." Unfortunately, the school administrators did not share my philosophy.

My breaking another player's stick became such a big issue because of my reputation. It was common knowledge that I was involved with drugs.

No one was hurt by my actions, but the administration was ready to take drastic measures against me. I was suspended for the first three games of the season. Additionally, my parents sent me to an inpatient psychiatric facility called Four Winds for anger management and substance abuse. The majority of the residents at Four Winds had serious mental health issues.

I was very upset about being suspended for three games, and even angrier that I was being sent away to a psychiatric facility. The night before I was supposed to go to Four Winds, I took a few swigs of Vodka that I stole from my parents and smoked the rest of the weed I had. Of course, I always take things to extremes, so I decided to steal my dad's car and go for a joy ride. It was raining on that November night in 2003, and there were a lot of leaves on the ground. I was speeding by the high school and lost control of my dad's car. I drove off the road and hit a tree so hard that I cut it in half. The airbags deployed and the car was totaled. Somehow, I came out of the car without a scratch.

I called my dad and he rushed to the crash site. I thought he was going to kill me, but this was one of those moments where my dad was too scared to be angry with me. He was relieved that I was alive and unharmed. He brought me home and sat down and talked with me. I was pretty shaken up by the accident. He knew I was under the influence and scared out of my mind, so he told me to go to sleep because we had to be up early the next morning to go to Four Winds.

The clinical team at Four Winds discharged me after five days because they said I did not fit the criteria needed to stay at their facility. My first game back would be at the West Genesee tournament in upstate New York. Much to my dismay, I was put on the third line. I finished my sophomore year on the first line, and now I was starting my junior year on the third line. In both hockey and lacrosse, things were getting worse for me each year. This was supposed to be the other way around. My life was progressing ass backwards.

The other team scored a goal when my line was on the ice, so we were benched. I was steaming, watching kids younger than I am getting more ice time than I was. When the period ended, we went into the locker room as the Zamboni came out to clean the ice.

I threw my stick and helmet across the locker room. My coach started yelling at me and said, "If you don't want to be here, then just get undressed and leave." Coaches say things like that all the time to their players, but I was in such a rage that I took it literally. I took off my jersey and started ripping off my equipment. My coach and the other players in the locker room were shocked at my behavior.

I put my street clothes on and stormed out of the locker room with my equipment. My father was away on business, so my mother attended the game alone. She came up to me and told me to get back in the locker room and put my equipment back on. It was the last period of the game and it would have been too late by the time I got back on the ice.

I calmed down and regretted removing my jersey. I should have listened to my coach without losing my temper. After the game, I went up to him and apologized for what I did. I told him I had to work on my anger and I didn't know why I kept acting like this. His response was not what I had expected. He told me that this was the last straw and that I was off the team.

I became so upset that I started to cry. My sadness quickly turned to anger and as I started to walk away, I threw my warm up jacket at my coach and cursed at him. If I wasn't off the team already, I definitely was now. I stormed out of Shove Park Ice Rink and on my way out, I punched out a glass window.

A few of my friends' fathers tried to calm me down. I started thinking about what it would be like to not be part of the Suffern Hockey team. Sports was my identity, especially hockey. In my mind, without sports, drugs was all I had left.

The administration gave me a ten-day suspension for throwing my warm up jacket at my coach and cursing at him, and I was suspended from the hockey team indefinitely. I was devastated. I had no plans of going back to school after my suspension. I thought to myself, If I wasn't on the hockey team, what was the point of going to school?

All of my best friends were on the team. We went to our coach's office every day during lunch to talk hockey. I was very close to my coach and he had always tried to help me since I was a little kid playing on the youth teams. My little brothers Johnny and K also played hockey and loved to go to all the Suffern Varsity Hockey games. I'll never forget the look on their faces as they both stood there in their Suffern Hockey sweatshirts when my mom told them I was no longer on the team. It was like losing a part of our family. During that time, all I did was use drugs. How did I get so lost?

I did end up going back to school after my ten-day suspension, but was suspended again just days later for coming to school under the influence of marijuana. I no longer used the tricks to mask my marijuana use. I didn't care anymore. I "hot boxed" the car with one of my friends and walked into school reeking of weed. Subconsciously, I wanted to get caught.

Things were worse than ever at home. I had been seeing a drug and alcohol counselor, Joseph Lanzone, since the beginning of the school year. My parents called an emergency meeting with him one Saturday morning. I was arguing with my parents during the entire ride. We pulled into his office parking lot, and I refused to get out of the car. My father came around and tried to pull me out, and that's when I snapped.

I was high on weed and Xanax and went into what some call a "xany rage." I threw a punch at my dad and we began fighting on the ground. Joseph came out and my mother told him to call 9-1-1. The Clarkstown Police showed up within minutes, but I had run away. They found me soon after and brought me to the crisis center in the back of a patrol car.

This was my first time in the back of a police car, but it certainly would not be my last. The staff at the crisis center in Pomona, New York, asked me a bunch of questions and eventually released me to my parents. They urged my parents to get a Person In Need of Supervision (PINS) Petition. PINS is for parents or guardians of troubled children. The court system can assist parents with their children who are out of control.

After I was suspended the second time for going to school under the influence of marijuana, I never returned. At the age of 16, I stopped going to school completely. I wanted to drop out. My plan was to live at home and sell and use drugs.

My parents were lost. They tried everything to guide me in the right direction and get me the help that I needed. They decided it was time to take drastic measures. They hired a treatment planning consultant to get me into some type of inpatient program. They asked me if I would go to a program willingly and I replied, "Absolutely not." Unbeknownst to me, they had already hired two ex-marines to bring me to a wilderness program.

In January of 2004, I went out one weekend with some of my friends. I came home late, and fell asleep on the couch watching the movie, *Reservoir Dogs*. At 5:00a.m., I was awakened by two ex-marines. They were hired by my parents as sober escorts. Their job was to bring me to a wilderness program called Second Nature in Atlanta, Georgia.

Whether I was willing or unwilling to go to Second Nature, these guys were going to get me from point A to point B regardless of my wishes. They explained to me what was going on and that I was going to a program to help me deal with my substance abuse and behavioral issues. They could see I was getting irritated and was looking for a way out. Then their body language and tone changed instantly.

One of the them told me I could do this the easy way or the hard way. He told me that some punk kid tried it the hard way last week and that he was probably still pulling the kitchen tile out of his teeth after they slammed his face into the floor.

My tone changed quickly from angry to sad and I began to cry. They saw right through me and told me to cut it out. I became angry again but went along willingly. My parents already had a bag packed for me, so we got in the car and left for the airport.

I was asking a lot of questions about where I was going, but they kept asking me about what was going on in my life and asking why I thought I ended up in such a bad spot.

We arrived at the airport, and I thought this was where we were going to part ways. I was wrong. They were with me all the way to the end of the trip. I sat in a middle seat between the two ex-marines for the duration of the trip.

We landed in Atlanta, Georgia, and I was handed off to two staff members from the wilderness program. They packed my stuff in the car, and off we went. They explained to me exactly where I was and what a wilderness program was all about. The first question I asked was, "How long will I be staying here, and when can I go home?" They told me they could not answer that question because the length of stay varied from person to person. In an effort to get me to comply with the rules, they told me that my behavior and willingness to participate in my recovery would help me move along in the program.

I would describe Second Nature Wilderness program as a therapeutic style boot camp. The staff members screamed and yelled at us often, and made us talk about our feelings. Attendees had to build their own tents to sleep in, cook their own food over a fire, and hike with 70 pound packs to various campsites. There were no bathrooms or showers.

When I arrived at the main office of Second Nature, I was given a large pack with clothes, food, boots, a personal tent, and some miscellaneous items. A staff member then drove me to see a doctor to get a physical. After I was cleared, I was driven to the camp site to meet up with my group.

On average, there were four staff members and twelve residents in each group. The staff would rotate each week. That meant the four staff members would be with us for a week straight. They set up their own staff tent in the middle of our individual tents.

When I got to the campsite, one of the counselors came over and introduced himself. He explained all of the rules and expectations. For the first week, I wasn't allowed to talk with any residents. I was only allowed to communicate with the counselors. I was assigned homework for both school and my recovery. I could not move into the next phase until I completed all of my work.

My first night there, I had to sleep in a tent with all of the counselors. I didn't get a second of sleep. I laid there all night through the thunderstorm. I just kept asking myself, "How did I end up here?" It was less than two years earlier that I had not even experimented with drugs or alcohol yet, and now I was in the middle of the woods in Georgia.

My experience at Second Nature was awful. I hated everything about it. There were a few brief moments where I was able to loosen up and have a good time, but I was miserable most of my stay.

There weren't any telephones, so I could only communicate with my parents through letters. I met with a therapist once a week, and he would tell me about his conversations with my parents.

I was a model resident at Second Nature. I wasn't going to do anything to lengthen my stay or prevent me from going home as soon as possible. I watched a few residents leave before me, and each of them were sent to a therapeutic boarding school.

No one would confirm how long I was staying or whether I was going home or to a therapeutic boarding school. I was just over seven weeks in when the new counselors came in to relieve their co-workers. When the new counselors rotated in, they brought our mail with them.

I got my mail, and went back to my tent to read my letters. I had a few letters from friends and family, but I was only looking for the letter from my parents. I saw it and ripped it open. I jumped for joy as I learned that I would be returning home to Suffern the next day. I would have to attend a special school for kids with behavioral issues in Rockland County for the remainder of my junior year, but I would be reintegrated into Suffern High School as long as I did my work and maintained good behavior.

The next day I was picked up at the campsite and brought back to the main office so I could shower and change my clothes. This was the first real shower I took in almost 8 weeks. It was such an amazing feeling. I flew back to New York and my family picked me up at the airport.

My experience at Second Nature wilderness program definitely changed me. I was ready to start over, or so I thought.

CHAPTER 15
No Second Chances

When I got back from Second Nature, I had the mindset that I was going to stay sober, do well in school, and get back into sports. I was coming home just in time for the start of lacrosse season.

My parents made me sign a home contract with some non-negotiable ground rules. First and foremost was sobriety. I was not allowed to use drugs or alcohol. I also had to see Joseph Lanzone, my drug and alcohol counselor, once a week. I had a curfew, had to maintain good grades, and give 100% effort in sports. Even though I was going to school on a different campus from Suffern High School, I was still technically a student there and would be eligible to participate in sports.

I met with my hockey coach and apologized for my actions. We put it behind us and started to move forward. I played in a summer and fall house league with the rest of the guys on the Suffern Hockey team. I worked with a private on-ice trainer to help me sharpen my skating and stick skills. Things were going really well.

My family, friends, and counselors were all extremely supportive of my getting back into lacrosse and hockey. Sports wasn't just my identity growing up; it was my life. Being able to channel my energy towards something positive would have been a big part of my recovery.

I picked up my lacrosse stick and started practicing in the backyard the day I returned home. I had a goal with a "Hector the Rejector" shot blocker attached to it so I could practice shooting at the corners. I had a new rebounder to practice my catching and throwing. I felt good. I hadn't smoked in two months and could feel the difference in my stamina. This season was going to be my best, and then...

Just before tryouts, I found out that the school administration decided it would be a better idea to suspend me for the entire lacrosse season of my junior year. My parents already knew about their decision but decided not to tell me, hoping the school administration would reconsider. I was devastated by the news.

At my hearing about the incident that occurred at the hockey tournament in West Genesee, the school administrators decided to kick me off the hockey team for the rest of the season and suspend me from school for ten days. At the time, I was unaware that they also decided to suspend me from the lacrosse team before the season even started.

They said that allowing me to play lacrosse would send the wrong message to the rest of the students. They believed that there needed to be consequences for my actions. Evidently, going to a psychiatric hospital, being kicked off the hockey team, getting suspended from school for ten days, going to a wilderness program for eight weeks, and seeing a drug and alcohol counselor weekly was not enough for them.

My counselor wrote a strongly worded letter asking the administration to reconsider their decision, emphasizing how vital this lacrosse season was for my recovery. We even got a letter from my counselor at Second Nature. They ignored the letters, the decision was final.

The assistant superintendent at the time, Brian Miele, was the administrator who made the final decision. My father pleaded with him, but he wouldn't budge. He was the one who was emphasizing that it would not be the right thing to allow me to play lacrosse because it would send the wrong message to the other students. To say that he communicated his decision to me and my parents in a rude and obnoxious manner would be a gross understatement.

Ironically, fast forward to May of 2014 when Brian Miele plead guilty to improperly reporting the certification of teachers in the Suffern School District, including his wife and daughter. He did this so they could get higher salaries. He was stripped of his license as a school administrator. His fraudulent activity cost taxpayers an estimated $2.6 million dollars. What kind of message did he think that sent?

I will never forget the feeling of seeing all the lacrosse players walking into school with their sticks and equipment on the first day of tryouts while I was banned from playing. I remember thinking that I would never be able to get out from under my reputation as a "bad kid".

When I was younger, my dad often spoke about reputation and how much it means in a person's life. He was right. The school wasn't willing to give me a chance to redeem myself. Most of my friends played lacrosse or baseball that spring sports season. After the school day ended, they went to practices or games. I went home.

I got a job working at the local golf course to keep myself busy and make some extra money to play poker. Texas Hold'em became really popular during this time and almost all of my friends played.

On days I didn't have work, I started hanging out with some of my older friends who had already graduated from high school but were still living in Suffern. I had no one else to hang out with. I would stay at their houses or sit in the back seat of the car while they all smoked weed. I was miserable.

I couldn't play sports and I couldn't party. Without both of these things, who was I? I was nothing. I had no purpose. On the day I received my 90-day sobriety coin, I threw in the towel. I had enough. I went out to a party that night and drank. A few hours went by and I threw down on a blunt. I relapsed on marijuana and alcohol that night and began my nightmare all over again. I kept it a secret and appeared to be in control for some time, but that never lasts long.

School was out for the summer, and I quit my job a few weeks after I started. All I did that summer was party, play hockey, play poker, and mess around with girls. I wasn't sure if the school was going to allow me to play hockey my senior year, but the leagues I was playing in during the summer and fall were not associated with the school. The summer of 2004 ended, and my senior year began.

CHAPTER 16
The Kiss of Death

When I came back from Second Nature Wilderness Program, the school district decided to send me to a special school for troubled kids. By the end of my junior year, I was back at the high school for the second half of the day.

It's a strange feeling walking into high school as a senior and realizing it will be your last first day of school for your high school career. Most of my older friends had gone away to college, so I was hanging out with my core group of friends. We were a close group of about 13 guys, with a few stragglers here and there. Every one of us was an athlete, but some had either quit, been cut from, or kicked off sports teams by the time we were seniors.

At the beginning of my senior year, I was maintaining decent grades and not getting in trouble. I was learning to fly under the radar. I was still smoking weed just about every day and partying on the weekends. I had given up the harder drugs, for the time being. Between my group of friends and a few other girls, we had multiple houses where we were able to throw parties. We rotated houses every weekend. My friend who lived up the street from me threw the craziest parties of all once a month. He always threw parties on Saturday nights. He had a big house with an unfinished basement that was perfectly set up for a rager. He had couches, tables, music, and a ping pong table for epic games of beer pong.

A lot went down at his parties. Many Suffern High School students lost their virginity at his house. When I got back from Second Nature, my friend threw one of his bangers. He always did his rounds on the upper floors to make sure no one was getting out of control. Since I had just gotten back from the wilderness program, a lot of girls had sympathy for me. I took full advantage of this. During that one house party, the host of the party walked in on me three separate times, with three different girls.

I wasn't the type of guy to seek out drunk girls and take advantage of them, especially since I was most likely wasted myself at every high school party I attended. To say that I never took advantage of a girl in high school would be a lie. It wasn't until I was a few years older that I realized what that can do to a girl. A friend of mine told me about some of things that she did in high school and how she regretted her actions when she became an adult.

She made it clear that she was never raped or forced to do anything against her will, but that being labeled a "slut" felt awful. She said that she started sleeping with guys because it made her popular and got her a lot of attention. Guys started calling and texting her all the time. In the end, all that attention made her feel worse about herself.

She started drinking more and was getting blackout drunk at parties. On some of these nights, she ended up doing things she would not normally do, and waking up with an awful feeling of regret.

I understand the mindset of the male popular athlete because I was one of them. I could sum up my focus in high school into four words. Girls, party, state championship. Starting around 8th grade, my friends and I always talked about going to high school parties, losing our virginity, and winning a state championship. All three of these can be part of a happy and healthy high school experience if done responsibly with a clear mind.

My focus here is on being a good man. For students, if you are at a high school party and you see a drunk girl that is not in her right mind and is about to make a big mistake, step up and do something about it. Don't be the guy who stands by and watches it happen, or even worse, a person who takes advantage of a drunk girl. Be the man who stops the other guy from taking advantage of an intoxicated girl; better yet, stop the girl from making a mistake, then get her a sober ride home.

As a senior, I was the victim of a bad girl, the worst girl. She had complete control over me. She made me feel all warm and fuzzy inside when I had her, but cold and sick when I didn't. I was willing to do anything and everything to have her. Her name, Oxycodone.

CHAPTER 17
The New Math... 1 Week Supply Equals 7 Years of Hell

One morning in the fall of 2004, I planned on meeting up with two of my friends before school to smoke. I spoke with one of my friends on the phone right before he came to pick me up and he said to me, "My sister got her wisdom teeth pulled. She got a prescription for 30 Oxycodone, but only took 2 of them. I stole the bottle." I was always down to try new drugs, but none of us had ever tried any kind of narcotic painkiller before. This was going to be a first for all of us.

I was already with another one of our friends, so the three of us met up and first smoked a blunt. We drove around smoking and talking about the Oxycodone we had. We weren't exactly sure what it was, but knew that a lot of people who used drugs wanted to get their hands on them. Until that time, I had tried marijuana, alcohol, cocaine, and Xanax. I suffered serious consequences because of these drugs, but none of these drugs were opioids. Before that day, I never realized that a person could actually fall in love with a drug.

We pulled into the parking lot of the high school about five minutes before the bell rang. My friend popped open the bottle and took out three pills. We each took one. I put the circular shaped white pill in my hand staring at the numbers 512 engraved on the pill. I threw the 5mg Oxycodone into my mouth and washed it down with my lemon lime Gatorade. I put Visine in my eyes, sprayed some cologne on my sweatshirt, and walked into school with my friends.

Five minutes went by, and I felt nothing. Ten minutes went by; I felt nothing. Fifteen minutes went by, nothing. Then around 20 minutes after I took my first opioid narcotic painkiller, I was sitting in the back row of math class when a euphoric feeling came over me. I started to itch, but it felt so good to scratch that itch. A tear watered out of my eye and rolled down my face. I wiped it away smiling. My face held that smile for the rest of the period. Combined with the potent skunk marijuana I was smoking, my first experience with Oxycodone left an indelible mark in my memory.

I laid my head down on my forearm sitting at my desk. This was the first time I could recall wishing the period would never end. I didn't want to move. The bell finally rang and I walked out into the hallway. I walked by one my friends and she said to me, "Steve, you look so high right now; go put Visine in your eyes before a teacher notices." I had already put in Visine to get rid of my red eyes, but it was no match for the power of Oxycodone. I met up with my other two friends who took the pills with me. They were both visibly messed up. One of them said to me, "This stuff is great," but it ended there for him. My other friend hated it because he said the pill made him nauseous. I was infatuated with this feeling and found it intoxicating. I told my friend I would give him $50 for the remainder of the bottle. He agreed and went out to his car at lunch time and gave it to me. The deal was sealed, and so was my fate.

I felt safe and secure knowing I still had 25 pills left to use. This new euphoria stayed with me for most of the school day. The final bell rang, and I went out to my friend's car and popped another one in my mouth as we waited in line with the rest of the seniors for the buses to leave. We drove to my friend Kris' house to play poker and smoke weed. I was wasted. I kept smoking because it was increasing the effects of the Oxycodone.

I started to feel dizzy, so I had one of my friends drive me home. Before I walked into the house, I threw up into the bushes. Unless you are an opioid addict, you will not understand how throwing up actually felt good to me. I was laughing as I was throwing up. Complete insanity. I walked into my house and hurried upstairs to my room. That day would forever change my life.

I had 24 pills left the next morning. I doubled it to four pills a day, finishing the bottle in six days. I called my friend, Dan, on day one and told him that I got my hands on Oxycodone. He flipped out and begged me to save him a few for when he came home from college during Thanksgiving break. I intended on doing just that, but I took all of them well before he returned from school.

My addiction to painkillers did not get out of control right away simply because I did not have easy access to them. I only used painkillers a few times my senior year. Every time I got my hands on them, it was a stolen prescription of Percocet or Vicodin from someone who was prescribed 30 pills and only took one or two. Why would a doctor prescribe 30 painkillers to someone who would probably only need a day or two's worth at most?

I could write an entire book on the prescription drug and heroin epidemic: how it started, who is responsible, how it could have been avoided, and what this country needs to get out of it. An in-depth conversation about this major public health issue needs to be brought to the public. Every time I speak and get to this part of my presentation, I stop my story and talk about this dangerous and deadly epidemic in America.

People are dying every day from prescription painkiller and heroin overdoses. For someone who does not have experience in this field or knowledge about this public health crisis, you might be thinking to yourself, "What do heroin overdoses have to do with doctors prescribing too many painkillers?" Well, it has absolutely everything to do with it.

The prescription painkiller epidemic started with big pharmaceutical companies such as Purdue Pharma marketing drugs including OxyContin as non-addictive. Doctors were starting to treat pain as a fifth vital sign and handing out opioid prescriptions as if it were candy on Halloween. Painkillers are opioids, just like heroin. They both attach to the same receptors in the brain. At the same time the prescription painkiller epidemic was on the rise, drug cartels saw an opportunity to make billions off of the heroin trade.

When you hear the tale of young people overdosing on heroin, the story will usually unfold in the same manner. The people who overdosed started out with Vicodin or Percocet. Maybe they broke a bone, had surgery, got their wisdom teeth pulled, or stole a prescription from someone who experienced one of the three. Soon they become addicted to these pills and the 5mg or 10mg pills with acetaminophen in them just aren't cutting it. So, they moved on to 30mg Oxycodone, sometimes referred to as Roxys or blues. These pills do not have acetaminophen in them, and this allows you to take more without seriously damaging your liver. Next on the hit parade is 80mg OxyContin. These big green goblins are on an entirely different level. The high is beyond anything you can imagine, and so are the withdrawals.

If the person has a legitimate prescription from a doctor, it will certainly not be enough to last a month once he or she becomes addicted. This forces us addicts to the street. Addicts will start to buy painkillers from dealers at an extremely high price. It becomes unaffordable, so addicts have no choice but to turn to a significantly cheaper drug, heroin. A person will usually start out snorting or smoking heroin and then finally progress to the deadly needle. Much of today's heroin is laced with a drug called Fentanyl. Heroin is made from the opium poppy plant. Fentanyl is a synthetic version that is made in labs and can be up to 100 times more powerful than heroin.

Dealers are lacing their heroin with Fentanyl to increase potency. The problem is that these dealers are not chemists, and often put in too much Fentanyl. This leads to overdoses and even death.

"My kid is a good kid, he will never end up strung out on heroin." This is a phrase I hear all too often. Although the majority of kids will not end up addicted to prescription painkillers or heroin, doing so has nothing to do with being a good or a bad kid. If you are able to drop the parental naivety and understand that everyone is vulnerable to this public health crisis, then there are a few things you can do to in terms of prevention. If anyone in your family, including you, is in a position where a doctor may prescribe prescription painkillers, stop and ask, "Do I really need this?" The truth is that America is full of people who are unwilling to deal with pain. There are plenty of people who can get by with just an over the counter medication after surgery, but they take painkillers because it was prescribed by a doctor. If it's prescribed by a doctor, then it must be safe, right? Wrong! The human brain does not know the difference between Oxycodone that was prescribed by a doctor and what is bought from a dealer off the street corner. If you are in a situation where you need to take painkillers, make sure you get rid of any left over. Most police departments have prescription drop boxes where you can bring unfinished prescriptions to be destroyed, no questions asked.

I am often asked the following question during the Q&A part of my program: "As a recovering addict, what would you do if you were in a situation where you had to take painkillers?" In July of 2015, I ran into this problem, and I will reveal how that unfolded later, when I discuss that part of my journey.

CHAPTER 18
Excommunicated

Even through all the madness going on in my life, I was able to keep things under control because I did not want to do anything to jeopardize my chances of playing on the varsity hockey team my senior year. We had a solid squad, certainly state championship material. The day before tryouts, I had a meeting with the principal, athletic director, and coaches of the varsity hockey team. My mother was at the meeting as well. My father could not attend because he was away on business.

The principal took charge of the meeting. This guy despised me, and I felt the same way about him. He started off by threatening to kick me off the team if I did one thing wrong. The entire meeting consisted of him telling me what a bad kid I was and that I should be filled with gratitude that they were even considering letting me play. My coaches didn't say much since it was out of their hands at this point. I remember the head coach calling me into his office after the meeting to ask me if I was okay. He saw how upset I was once the meeting ended.

Knowing that I was a troubled kid, I felt that asking me to exhibit perfect behavior with no screw ups the entire season was to set me up for failure. I am an emotional person, and sometimes I let my emotions get the best of me, but I never once hit another student or damaged any school property.

I was no longer excited for my last season of hockey. I had a bad feeling about it. The possibility of being kicked off the team yet again gave me intense anxiety. I could not imagine sitting in the stands watching my friends, most of whom I had known since kindergarten, take the ice without me.

The first day of tryouts went well. It was all skating and drills. Then I walked in the second day, which was the blue-white scrimmage. The coach split up the roster into two teams and we played against each other. He posted the lines on the locker room door. I was not on the first, second, or third line. I was on the fourth line; the last line. There are three forwards to a line, and there weren't even three of us. He put me on a line with the worst player on the team to try to get inside my head. He succeeded.

I thought to myself, "This is it. I am going to be benched for the entire season until I can't take it anymore and quit or do something stupid and get kicked off the team." Based on the meeting I had with the administration two days earlier, I was convinced this was them sending me the message that they didn't want me on their team.

I arrived at Sport-O-Rama Ice Rink an hour before practice that day, so most of the coaches hadn't arrived yet. I was taught to remove myself from a situation when I feel myself losing control, so I did just that. I walked out of the ice rink very upset and got in my car. I called my drug counselor, but he did not answer the phone. Then I called Conor, and he answered. We talked for about a minute as I drove around the parking lot. He talked me down and told me to go back inside. He told me that come game time, I would be back on top. I didn't believe that, but I went inside and started to put on my equipment.

I was all dressed and ready to go before the scrimmage started. My coach walked in the locker room and asked me why I left the rink? One of the other coaches saw me get in my car. I told him I was upset but now I was fine. I barely touched the ice at all during the entire scrimmage.

At the end of the scrimmage, I went up to the coaches and told them how I felt about the way I was being treated and judged. I felt certain expectations were unfair. I walked out of the rink, and that would be my last day as a Suffern Hockey player. The next day in school, I was told that I was not allowed to go to practice and that the administration was going to decide whether or not they were going to allow me to play on the team.

The following day I was called into my coach's office. He was sitting there with the athletic director, who proceeded to tell me that they decided

I was not allowed to play on the hockey team. When I asked why, the reason given was that I left the ice rink and that they warned me if I did anything wrong I would be kicked off the team. I left the ice rink to cool down because I was so upset about being put on the fourth line as a senior when I was on first line as a sophomore. I used the skills I learned at Second Nature and with my drug counselor. I never even left the parking lot. This gave the administration the excuse they wanted to get rid of me.

I ran to my car and sped out of the school parking lot. Deservedly, I immediately lost my school driving privileges for speeding. For this, I cannot say I blame them. The school put in speed bumps the next week. (One of the security guards called them the Steve bumps.) I felt like my world was crashing down on me. My parents were in a meeting with the administration when I sped out of the parking lot. They had to cancel the meeting and come home.

I drove to a gas station in New Jersey to pick up cigarettes. I had quit smoking cigarettes in the summer, but I needed one that day. When I got home, my parents looked helpless, as did I. We didn't know what to do. I was no longer part of the Suffern Hockey family. That's what it was, a family. To me, it was much more than a sports team. Even worse for my mother was that she was practically Mrs. Suffern Hockey. She was in charge of fundraising, apparel, and the annual golf outing. She secured brand new jerseys the year before and spearheaded the $50,000 fundraiser for our hockey locker room which was completed my senior year. I never stepped foot in that locker room.

Just when I thought there was no way out, my parents had an impossible idea, and what we did next will go down in history as one of the craziest moves in high school sports history. A real "Friday Night Lights" situation.

CHAPTER 19
The Reason Why

Chapter 4 is titled "It Happened for A Reason," I was cut from the Ramapo Saints travel hockey team in 6th grade and ended up trying out for the Clarkstown Capitals instead. I made the team and had an amazing experience. I was the leading scorer that year. Our team was so much better than the Ramapo Saints team that cut me that they wouldn't agree to play us because they knew it would be a bloodbath. That's what happened. Here's the "everything happens for a reason" part.

Rich Willows was one of the head coaches of the Clarkstown Capitals travel team I played for in 6th grade. His son, Rich Jr., was on the team. Fast forward six years and Rich Jr. was playing for the Clarkstown North High School varsity hockey team, and his father, was an assistant coach. There were also four other kids on the Clarkstown North varsity hockey team who I played with when I was on the Clarkstown Capitals. Clarkstown is a few towns over from Suffern and the two schools were hockey powerhouses and became rivals in varsity ice hockey. They were always the two best teams in Rockland County.

A few weeks before tryouts for the Suffern varsity ice hockey team, my mother ran into Rich Willows at Sport-O-Rama. He asked her how everything was going with Suffern. She told him that they were still giving me a hard time and were going to make me tryout for the team again as a senior. Rich was very upset at hearing this and said, "I wish he could just come play for us at North."

Once it was confirmed that I was not allowed to be part of the Suffern hockey team, my mother remembered her former conversation with Rich, and my father called him and relayed what had transpired. He told Rich that I wanted to play hockey for Clarkstown North High School. He asked Rich how we could make that happen? Rich said he would love for me to come play for their team and that there were two ways for this to become a reality. I either had to move to the Clarkstown School District, or I could pay the district to be a student. My parents first opted to enroll me by paying the district. A problem arose at registration once the Clarkstown School District was made aware that I had an IEP (Individualized Education Plan) and was part of the BOCES program. Clarkstown would not accept my application since the cost of having an IEP and being in the BOCES program would be much greater than the amount they were charging me to enroll. The Director of Special Education at Clarkstown was adamantly against it.

We had to now try the second option of moving into the school district. Since the Director of Special Education knew we were trying to get me enrolled and was fighting it, my parents hired an attorney, who specialized in education law.

My Dad found an apartment in the Clarkstown School District so we could claim residency there. Once this was done, we went back to register me as a student. My parents told the school to contact our attorney with any questions or concerns. Once my father proved his residency, they had no choice but to allow me to enroll, and the varsity hockey team was more than happy to have me. Things took a strange turn when they figured out that my IEP mandated that I be a part of the BOCES program which was housed at Suffern High School. I would be a Clarkstown North student, but I would attend Suffern High School. I lived with my Dad in Clarkstown and he drove me to Suffern High School every day. I was thrilled! I could play hockey for Clarkstown North, but I could stay at my original high school with my friends.

I had to keep everything we were doing a secret until our plan was set in stone. My parents got all of this done in a week. Once my enrollment was confirmed, I went to my first practice. I already knew most of the guys on the team and was friends with some of them when I played travel hockey.

The coaches met with me after a few practices and told me that I was officially on the team. They emphasized how I had to keep a low profile because the Suffern administration was going to be gunning for me. My parents gave me the same advice.

It was a strange feeling knowing that I would be competing against Suffern, where so many of my close friends played.

The week before the season officially began, I walked into Suffern High School wearing my Clarkstown North hockey warm up suit. Many people were confused by this. There was no way I could be playing for Clarkstown as a student at Suffern. Yet, I was doing just that. It was the talk of the school for the rest of the season.

At lunchtime, I was called into the assistant principal's office. The entire Suffern administration was in there waiting for me. They started hammering me with questions asking if this was some type of joke. I told them that it wasn't. I was officially on the Clarkstown North hockey team, and would be playing against Suffern come January. Then I said, "If you have any further questions, you can contact my attorney," and I walked out. The looks on their faces were priceless.

We got word that the Clarkstown School District hired a private investigator to check that I came out of the door at my father's newly rented apartment. We originally thought that we could simply rent the apartment to claim residency, but we had to live there or else I could be thrown out of the school and off the team.

We played against Suffern twice that year. The first time we played was at Suffern's home rink, Sport-O-Rama. A few hours before the game, my parents received a call from my coach telling them I was not eligible to play in the game because I was not present in gym class. The Suffern athletic director who was also my gym teacher, called the Clarkstown North athletic director and told her I was not in class. This was a complete lie. Luckily, I had a few close friends who had great reputations in the school and vouched for me and said I was absolutely in gym class that day. Things like this happened all season. I can't overemphasize the value and importance of a positive reputation. Your reputation follows you everywhere.

Conor, who was the captain of the varsity baseball team, got called down to the office one day. He sat in a room with the school administration and School Resource Officer (SRO) as they watched a video of someone doing donuts with a car and ripping up the infield of the junior varsity baseball field.

Conor said they immediately started blaming me for it. They were trying to get him to turn on me saying things such as, "Doesn't this just grind your gears Conor? That is your field out there." Conor told me that they were certain it was me ripping up the field in my mom's white Cadillac Escalade. He told me it could not have been more obvious that it wasn't an Escalade; it was a Rav-4.

Conor left the office and tracked me down in school. He was laughing hysterically when he approached me and told me how ridiculous the entire situation was. He said, "So there pretty much was a sign in the corner of the screen that said Stephen Hill is not in this car, and they covered it up with their hands." Obviously, he was being sarcastic, but he made his point. The administration was doing everything to try to prevent me from playing the game I loved.

After the nonsense was cleared up, I got ready for my game against Suffern. I pulled up to the rink on the bus with my team an hour before the game and the line of fans was already around the corner. The game was sold out that night. I was not ready for the emotional rollercoaster of that evening. Hate, anger, adrenaline, excitement, revenge, sadness, happiness; all were part of me that night.

We lost 3-1, and I took four penalties. It was a terrible feeling. A few weeks later I got my revenge when we played against them again at our home rink at the Palisades Mall. My former coach on the Clarkstown Capitals, Mickey Carroll, pulled me aside before I took the ice. He told me to take the angry look off my face and smile. He told me to play my game, and focus on the scoreboard. I played on the same line with his son, Mickey Jr.

During my first shift, I took the puck end to end, weaving in and out of my former teammates on Suffern. As I approached the goal, I could see the defenseman and goalie cheating towards me, willing to do whatever it took to make sure I didn't score. I took full advantage of this and passed the puck across the crease to a wide open Mickey Carroll. He slammed the puck in the net and we went wild. We beat Suffern 5-1 that day, and I got a few points on the board. That was one of the greatest days of my life.

The title of the newspaper article in The Journal News the next day was "Rams Pound Mounties." The article started out highlighting my end to end rush and assist to Mickey Carroll. I was quoted in the article as well. I taped the article to my chest and wore my Clarkstown North varsity jacket to Suffern High School the next day. One of my teachers told me to take the article off my chest or the school would try to get me in trouble. She took the article and posted it on the wall in her classroom.

It looked like we were going to play against Suffern in the section championship, but we lost in the semifinals in triple overtime. I was devastated. Suffern ended up winning the section, but they lost their next game in the state quarter finals. High school hockey was over for all of us.

I am forever grateful to my Clarkstown North teammates, their families, the coaches, and the athletic director for allowing me to play for the Rams my senior year of high school. My teammates could have easily said they didn't want a player who was thrown off the Suffern team to play with them. The parents could have easily said that they didn't want some outsider coming in and taking a spot that belonged to one of their kids. The coaches could have said that they already have a full roster and didn't need a player who was excommunicated from his hometown. The Clarkstown North High School administration could have easily not allowed this to happen. The athletic director at Clarkstown North, Tess Brogan, was very supportive throughout the season. I believe that I would not have graduated high school if Clarkstown North had not taken me in as one of their own. Playing on that team kept me focused, out of trouble, and most importantly, in school. The parents of the 2004-2005 Clarkstown North varsity hockey team wrote several letters to me and my parents, but one in particular stood out.

"We all tend to get caught up in the game, but we forget the amount of effort these kids have put in, in order to be able to play a sport at this level.

The problem is that sometimes we think it's just a sport and not a vehicle for life's lessons. When Stephen joined our team, there was skepticism by the parents as to why we would take in a castaway from another team. Why should we take a chance and lose a slot for one of our kids?

Well, I think we all learned that there are no castaways. There are kids who get into difficult situations and need a new opportunity. Stephen proved this point to the parents and teammates in his Clarkstown North Hockey family.

We are very proud to have played with Stephen. *He is intense on the ice. He plays with everything he's got. He will find his way in life despite the obstacles that some might throw at him. You should feel great about how you and he handled a difficult situation. We wish you all the best."*

-   *Phil Samuels*

Phil is the father of Jeff Samuels, the captain of the 2004-2005 Clarkstown North Hockey team, Honorable Mention All Section and All County.

My parents also had a letter published in the local newspaper for Rockland County, The Journal News.

"We want to thank the Clarkstown High School North varsity hockey coaching staff for believing that our 17-year-old son, Stephen, deserved a second chance. We especially want to thank Rich Willows, assistant varsity hockey coach, for immediately recognizing that a kid who had devoted his entire young life to a sport shouldn't be denied the opportunity to play his senior year.

We also want to thank Head Coach Ken Warger, Coach Dave Lynch and Athletic Director Tess Brogan, who had the courage and compassion to welcome a new kid on the team and immediately make him feel like he belonged. Thanks, too, to the Clarkstown North Hockey Team for, as Coach Warger said, "accepting Stephen as one of your own." And to the incredible North parents who accepted us and made us feel welcome when we were just about to give up on people, thank you.

We also want to thank those staff members at Suffern High School who cared and supported Stephen through it all, especially Jason Kahn, the BOCES social worker, the Suffern hockey players who went to bat for

their teammate and then encouraged him to stay in school and play for North. We also want Stephen to know how very proud of him we are. What a life lesson you learned: Life is not always fair; take what is given to you and make the best of it. You did that, and we are proud."
-   *Kevin & Laurie Hill*

Reading these letters brings tears to my eyes and mixed emotions as well. I feel gratitude for everyone from the Clarkstown North family that took me in, but sadness that I didn't get a chance to play my junior or senior year with the Suffern Hockey boys with whom I played with since childhood.

After the hockey season ended, my father got rid of the apartment and moved back home. I was actually given the choice to play lacrosse for Clarkstown North or Suffern, but I decided not to play for either. Clarkstown North did not have a great lacrosse team that year, and I didn't really know anyone on the team. There was no way I was playing for Suffern, so I quit.

I am not shy about throwing blame onto the school administration for the way they treated me, but I still have to take responsibility for my own actions. I went back and met with my former Suffern hockey coach recently, and we played the "what if" game for a while. He wasn't part of the unethical tactics used by the administration, and he had nothing to do with my not being allowed to play lacrosse my junior year when I returned from the wilderness program. Could he have done things differently? Yes, but I could have as well. My reputation caused most of this to happen. If I weren't abusing drugs, my behavior would not have been so threatening. At the end of the day, I let drugs and alcohol get in the way of my success in sports and academics and hurt countless people along the way.

Towards the end of May of 2005, a friend who was three years older than I was came home from college with some pills. They were called OxyContin. I had heard of Vicodin, Percocet, and Lortab, but never OxyContin. He told me that taking this one pill was more powerful than taking eight Perc 10's (10mg Percocet) all at once. He handed me a green pill that said OC on the front and 80 on the back. This was an 80mg

OxyContin. He broke the pill in half and told me taking a whole one would be too much for my first time. I took the half, but didn't feel the effects right away, so I made him give me the other half. After I took the second half of the 80mg OxyContin, the first half kicked in, hard. Within twenty minutes I felt the full effects. I was barely coherent.

I sat in the passenger's seat all day driving around smoking weed. I felt like my body was molded to the seat. It was insane. I was high for twelve hours straight on just one pill. I wanted more, but he only had that one pill and said he couldn't get more until he went back to school. I searched high and low for an OxyContin connection, but was unable to find anyone who had the magic pill.

Senior prom came around and more trouble awaited me. Since I was no longer a student at Suffern High School, the administrators continued to make sure I could not attend, even as a date of a student. Because my girlfriend was a sophomore and not a senior, she couldn't bring me as her date. Once again, I had to figure a way to work out a tenuous situation. Since senior students are allowed to bring guests from other schools as a date, I was able to persuade a girl in my senior class to put me down on paper as her date. A friend of mine did the same for the sophomore girl who was to be my date.

The day after senior prom, I was supposed to take part in my first large scale drug deal. I was 17 years old and had saved $10,000 from selling weed. The plan was for me to front the money for 5 pounds of low grade marijuana. My friend, "C", was going to buy the five pounds from his connection at college. Then another friend, "G", had someone who was going to buy all five pounds for $16,000. We were going to split the $6,000 profit three ways.

"C" said that his dealer would only meet him alone. So, I gave him the money, and off he went. A few hours later he came back, empty handed. He told me and "G" that he was robbed at gunpoint. I put every dollar I made selling weed that year into that one drug deal, and lost it all.

This is the common theme for dealing drugs. Young guys get attracted to the fast, easy money. But just as easy and fast as it comes in, it goes out. Money made in the drug trade isn't real. It was not until I got sober and started working a legitimate job that I learned about the value of a dollar. There is a line Ray Liotta says in Martin Scorsese's *Goodfellas* that really stuck with me in my bad days. Ray Liotta is playing the real life mobster, Henry Hill (no relation), when he proclaims, "The working man is a sucker." My father hated that line. It made him sick the first time I said it to him. Now it makes me sick when I hear it.

I graduated from Clarkstown High School North; at least that what it reads on my diploma. My parents asked the Suffern administration if I could walk at the Suffern High School graduation with all of my friends. Guess what their answer was. "ABSOLUTELY NOT, HE IS NOT A SUFFERN HIGH SCHOOL STUDENT!" We didn't fight them or find a way around it for this one. I could have walked at Clarkstown's graduation, but I opted out.

Some people in Suffern will read or hear about this chapter in my book and be upset. Being labeled a "bad kid" and having so many people against you can give a kid a big push in the wrong direction. I do express my opinions, but I mostly just restate the facts. I take full responsibility for my actions, but I believe that many people in the school district did not act in my best interests.

CHAPTER 20
Busted

I ended up going to Morrisville State College in New York with one of my friends from Suffern. There wasn't much of a social life at Morrisville and I found the campus to be boring. We were about 30 minutes from Syracuse University where two of my close friends went to school. We went up to visit a few weeks after the first semester began. A girl from Suffern that was a year older got us into a frat party. I loved it. We went to a football game the next day and had a great time. The next weekend I went down to West Virginia University to visit two more friends who went to school there. That place was crazy. The amount of drinking and drugging going on at that campus was unbelievable.

I failed out of school by the end of October and moved back home. I was dating a younger girl since the winter of my senior year. She broke up with me soon after I failed out of college.

I picked up right where I left off. I began selling and using drugs again, but now I was 18 years old. I wasn't a minor anymore. I started selling more than just marijuana. I was selling cocaine and Xanax too.

Towards the end of my senior year and the summer going into my first semester of college, the Ramapo Police Street Crimes Unit began to show a presence in my community. Kids my age and older were getting pulled over by unmarked police vehicles on the weekends.

It became well known that there were two Dodge Intrepids, a gold and blue one, as well as a silver Chevrolet Impala, that had plain clothes officers and detectives patrolling the streets looking to nail high school and college kids for drugs. Of course, they paid closer attention to the people who were dealing the drugs.

Just before Christmas of 2005, I left my parents' house with three of my friends. We drove to a party and dropped off a few bags of weed. We had two blunts rolled and sparked them up as we pulled off the street. As soon as we made a right turn, a marked Ramapo Police car appeared behind us. After about 30 seconds of being tailed, the red and blue lights became illuminated. My friend pulled over immediately. We didn't have any drugs except for the two blunts we were smoking. We put them out and I ate them as soon as the lights went on. We didn't have anything illegal in the car, but we also knew that this wasn't an ordinary pullover.

The uniformed officer pulled up behind us, but did not get out of his car. A few seconds later the silver Chevrolet Impala and gold Dodge Intrepid came flying up the street with their red lights flashing. They blocked us in and four plain clothes officers hopped out of the two vehicles. They pulled all four of us out of the car and began searching. They even called in the K-9 Unit. The police did not find anything that night, so they had to let us go; however, it was clear to me that I was being watched.

A few weeks after New Year's I was pulled over again leaving my house. I had 4 individual grams of marijuana on me. I didn't pull over right away because I was trying to pull the marijuana out of the bags and eat it to get rid of the evidence. That was what my dealer taught me to do. It was too difficult to do and the cop ended up blocking me in and ripping me out of the car on to the ground. In January of 2006, I was arrested for the first time. I was charged with resisting arrest and unlawful possession of marijuana.

I was brought down to the Ramapo Police Headquarters where they took a mugshot, fingerprinted me, and gave me a court date. I was then released to my father. He was furious, but somewhat relieved. He had hoped that getting arrested would whip me into shape. He couldn't have been more wrong.

My parents tried getting me to go back to school at Delhi College. We went through orientation and the entire admissions process. Just as my parents were about to leave, I told them that this was a complete waste of time and money and that I was going to fail out. I knew I wasn't ready for college, and my parents did too. I packed my stuff and went home with my parents. They knew that if I stayed at home I would get into trouble, and that is exactly what happened.

Less than a month later, I was arrested again with six of my friends. We were throwing parties and hanging out in my friend's empty house. His parents had moved out, but they had not sold the house yet. On a cold Friday night in February of 2006, multiple officers and detectives raided my friend's house. We were sitting around watching "Wedding Crashers" when I saw cops running into the house. One of the detectives was a close family friend of my parents. He knew just about every guy in that house and although he was amped up to do a raid at first, he had a look of complete disappointment when he saw who was in the house. That night, we were all charged with criminal possession of marijuana. I was also charged with criminal possession of a controlled substance. I had 11 Vicodin in my pocket.

The next day my father took me to see a criminal defense attorney, David Goldstein. Goldstein and my parents recommended that I go to an inpatient treatment program both to try and get better and to show the court that I was getting help for my substance abuse issues. More importantly, I really did need help. I checked into the Caron Foundation in Wernersville, Pennsylvania. The Caron Foundation is a top of the line treatment facility that cost my parents a lot of money, $30,000 to be exact. Insurance did not cover 1 cent. Today, insurance companies are more willing to cover some of the costs at an inpatient treatment facility. Unfortunately, I cannot say the same for residential costs at an extended care program. Insurance will not cover any of those costs.

I stayed at Caron for 28 days, then came back home. The level of care that I received at Caron was amazing. I learned a lot about myself, addiction and recovery. My parents naively thought that if they were paying this amount of money at one of the top treatment facilities in the country, I would have been cured when I came out. This could not have been farther from the truth. We had a lot to learn, and this was just the beginning. 28 days just was not enough for me. I needed more time, a lot more time.

When I came home from Caron I started going to support groups including Alcoholics Anonymous and managed to put together some sober time. I leased a car and got a job working at Minisceongo Golf Course. Things were going pretty well for me, but all of my friends living at home were drinking and smoking. After a few months of staying sober, I gave in. I started slacking off at work and calling in sick. I was eventually fired. I had a car payment and drug habit to support, so I started selling weed again. I decided that I wasn't going to sell any hard drugs because of the heat (police presence) it brought on me. I was introduced to a new weed connection and opened up shop.

I tried again to go to school in the Fall of 2006. I started at Dominican College which was about a 15-minute commute from my parents' house. Again, I failed out in less than two months. It was clear that I was not ready to go to college, so my parents helped me find a job. I ended up being employed as an assistant loan officer at a mortgage bank. My mother knew the owner's wife, and he was willing to give me a chance. I went through a two-week training course with a few other people who were trying to become loan officers. I was only going to be an assistant.

I was abusing painkillers on a daily basis at this point. I was taking about ten perc 10's a day when I was first hired at the mortgage bank. Even with my drug habit, I started off strong. I assisted several different loan officers making cold calls, scheduling appointments, and writing out mortgage loans.

The mortgage bank was located in Floral Park, Queens. I was commuting over an hour each way from my parents' house. Driving in the morning was dangerous. There were several times where I would wake up still high on Percocet from the night before, pop a few more, and jump in the car to drive to work. I can remember on several occasions having to pull over and throw water on my face to try to wake myself up because I kept nodding off behind the wheel.

Luckily, I was able to help get my friend, Jason, a job working there. We carpooled most of the time, but there was no way I could maintain my job at the mortgage bank with this drug habit. Although the painkillers were not really affecting my job performance, I started missing work more often. I called in sick and used my grandfather's illness as an excuse for why I could not come into work. I told my boss that there was no one else home to help my grandmother take care of my grandfather. Some of the time, this was true. I used it as an excuse quite often and was given a warning about missing too many days, but I kept calling out of work anyway.

Waking up high almost every morning and trying to work an honest job that paid $12/ hour with over an hour commute was not appealing to me. In fact, I was losing money because I could make much more selling weed if I stayed home. Waking up with an addicted brain and trying to convince myself to get out of bed and go to work was an everyday struggle. There was one day I wish I never called out sick. This was a missed work day that I would regret for years to come.

CHAPTER 21
Stay to the Right

On January 30th, 2007, I made a decision that would change my life forever. I was on my way to work when I decided I could not go any further. Even when I managed to get out of bed, get dressed for work, and get in the car, it was still a struggle the entire ride. My disease was in full control at this point. I was taking at least 100 mgs of Percocet and smoking 5 blunts a day. The voice in the back of my head would convince me that, "The working man is a sucker."

I stopped at a rest stop on the Palisades Parkway and left a message for my boss that I would not be coming into work that day. I was nodding out at the wheel, so I turned around and headed home. I got back into bed and went to sleep. A few hours later, I got a call from my friend, Chris, asking me if I wanted to go four wheeling in the trails by Kakiat Park. I didn't have my own four-wheeler, but Chris's friend, Punch, had a two-man four-wheeler we could ride. I popped a few more Percocet and met up with them.

We drove to the trails and started heading up the mountain. Chris was on the single four-wheeler and knew the trails well. I remember him telling Punch to stay behind him. I was on the back of the two-man four-wheeler with Punch. Chris was leading the way and everything was going smoothly. Punch didn't know the trails well, so it was important that he followed Chris. The trails weren't wide enough for Punch to pass Chris until we got to the bottom of a cliff.

We reached a point where the trails opened up. If we had gone up the cliff and stayed to the right as Chris did, we would have driven down safely.

If we had gone up the left side of the cliff, we would have flown off a steep drop when we get to the top. When Punch and I approached the bottom of the cliff, he gunned the throttle full blast and we started flying up the left side of the cliff. When we reached the top, we flew right over. The four-wheeler fell forward, and I was flung off the back and down the cliff. After a few seconds airborne, I hit the ground hard and tumbled about twenty feet down the cliff. My helmet came flying off as I plummeted to the bottom. If I didn't wear a helmet that day, there is a good chance I would not be alive today.

I only remember bits and pieces of what happened after the crash fall. I think I blacked out for a few seconds, but was awakened by Punch screaming in agony. I looked over at him and saw him rolling on the ground holding his shoulder. He broke his collarbone. The bone had not pierced, but you could see the broken bone protruding from the inside.

I looked up and saw his four-wheeler wedged precariously into a tree about twenty feet above us. If it fell out of the tree, it could fall and crush both of us and we would likely be killed. My head was pounding. I felt the back of my head and saw that my hand had blood on it. I went to wipe the blood off on my pants. When I picked my hand up again, there was significantly more blood on it. I couldn't figure out where the blood came from.

Chris ran over and stood above me. He stared at me and his face turned pale, full of fear. I do not remember saying this, but he told me I said, "I either have a really bad Charley Horse or I broke my leg." With a shaky voice he said, "Don't move, I am going to get help." He called 9-1-1 and drove his four-wheeler out to the street to meet the paramedics so he could show them where in the woods we had the accident.

Part of the reason Chris turned pale white when he looked at me was that he thought I broke my back. Somehow, the seat came off the four-wheeler, and I landed directly on top of it. Because of the way the seat is shaped, it arched my back in a grotesque way. I wish that was the only reason he was so concerned.

The blood on my hand came from a compound fracture of my right femur. My thigh bone was cracked in half and jutted out of my body through my jeans. The femur bone is the biggest bone in the human body and the hardest bone to break. I had never broken a bone before that day. I guess I am truly a go big or go home, all or nothing type of guy.

Chris flagged down the ambulance on the street and brought them to me in the woods. What I remember most about that day was being colder than I ever was before. It was in the middle of the winter, I was not dressed very warmly, I was not moving and was losing a lot of blood.

After about half an hour, Chris returned with three paramedics and one Ramapo police officer. They were trying to figure out the best way to get me out of there. I could not understand what the three paramedics were saying because they were Orthodox Jews speaking in Hebrew or Yiddish.

Nothing was being done until two of my childhood friends came to my rescue. Justin Gelband and David Salembier were my classmates since elementary school and also happened to be working as EMT's. They came running down the hill and got right to work. There was some talk about having a helicopter air lift me out of the woods, but there were too many trees around. David lived down the road from the crash site and rushed home to get his Suburban. He backed his truck up into the woods as far as he could.

At this point, I really did not feel any pain. My body was in shock, but that would all change as soon as I was moved onto the stretcher. I was carried up the hill and put into the back of David's Suburban. Now I was really feeling the pain as his truck rocked back and forth on the way out of the woods. I was finally moved out of his suburban and into the back of an ambulance. I was screaming and crying in agonizing pain and was immediately hit with a dose of morphine.

The rest of the day is a blur. I do not remember anything after the first injection of morphine. The next thing I knew I was waking up in the post-op room after surgery. My father told me about the phone call he received from the hospital at work. They told him his son was in a bad four wheeling accident and broke his leg. At first, he thought they might have the wrong information because we did not own a four-wheeler, only a dirt bike. But he knew that if one of his four sons were in the hospital, it was without a doubt me.

I was in the hospital for ten days after my surgery, mostly because I lost so much blood. I was not in a cast. The surgeon, Dr. Rubin, inserted a titanium rod through my hip and down my leg, ending at my knee. She had to insert a screw into my knee to hold the rod in place.

I was in excruciating pain, so the doctor had me hooked up to a morphine drip. I was pressing the button over and over again trying to get more morphine. I knew the drip was on a timer and that I could only get more after a certain period of time, but I still pressed it non-stop hoping to override the system.

Since I was addicted to painkillers at the time of my accident, the amount of morphine the nurses gave me was not enough to help with the pain because I had built up a tolerance. I called one of my friends and told him to bring more Percocet to the hospital. I was lucky that I had my own room throughout my stay at the hospital. I watched the HBO TV Series *The Wire* on my portable DVD player and popped painkillers along with the morphine drip. I had a catheter and was so backed up from all the medication they were giving me that I did not have to use the bathroom for the first week.

The first time I got out of bed was one of the most painful experiences of my life. I was screaming in pain. My leg felt like it was going to fall off after every hobble on the crutches. After I was discharged, I stayed in a wheelchair for about four months. I used crutches only when I had to. On April 20, 2007, I had to use crutches in order to get up to the podium and give a reading from the Corinthians at my grandfather's funeral at Sacred Heart Church in Suffern. My grandfather, Mario, suffered from Parkinson's Disease for a long time. He was a kind, decent, and hard-working man. He had an amazing voice. My family likes to watch the video of him and my mother's Uncle Tony singing "Oh Holy Night" on Christmas Eve. He is greatly missed.

Dr. Rubin gave me a two-week supply of 5mg Percocet for the pain from my injury. That wasn't nearly enough for me. The 100mgs of Percocet I was taking a day wasn't cutting it anymore either.

I remembered the pill my friend gave me about a year earlier, OxyContin. I was high for 12 hours on this pill the first time I took it. I began asking around to see if anyone had an OxyContin connect. I got a call back from my friend, Matt, who knew a guy with a prescription for 120, 80mg OxyContin pills every month. Matt picked me up after he got off work and drove me to his connect's house. He lived just a five-minute drive down the road. The connection turned out to be my friend's boss at the pizzeria where he worked. For security reasons, I wasn't allowed to go inside, so I gave my friend $150 for five pills. A few minutes later he came out with his boss, who introduced himself to me and gave me his number. He told me I could call him anytime.

Instead of popping the pills in my mouth like I always did, my OxyContin dealer told me to scrape off the time release, break the pill down into a powder, and snort lines of it. He told me I wouldn't regret it. In more ways than one, that was the understatement of the decade. I absolutely loved it. The high was instantaneous. I broke the green 80mg pill up into ten lines, and snorted one every half hour. I smoked multiple blunts as I sat back in my room and binge watched *The Wire*.

I would never take an OxyContin by mouth ever again after that night. I fell in love with snorting them. Having the back of my throat coated with Oxy as I swiftly took a big puff of a Marlboro Light became my favorite thing to do, and I did it all day, every day. OxyContin wasn't like Percocet; it was significantly more powerful. Before I got addicted to OxyContin, I never really experienced opioid withdrawals while I was taking Percocet. Although both Percocet and OxyContin are just brand names for the drug Oxycodone, they were immensely different.

I started off snorting about a pill and a half a day when I began abusing OxyContin. I was paying $30 a pill from my regular connection, and sometimes more when I got them from other sources. As my addiction to OxyContin progressed, I began finding more dealers so I would never run out. In the summer of 2007, I ran out of OxyContin. I called my friend, Pete, who was selling weed for me at the time to see if he knew anyone who had OxyContin. He said he didn't, but he could get me something else just as good for much cheaper.

I had no idea what Pete was talking about. What drug could be just as good as OxyContin but was also much cheaper?

CHAPTER 22
There's no Hero in HEROin

I had to meet up with Pete that day anyway to collect $400 he owed me and to give him another ounce of weed. My parents were out, so he came to my house. I went out to the street and walked up to his car window on one crutch. I handed him another ounce of weed in a brown paper bag, and he gave me the $400 he owed me in an envelope. He told me there was a present inside at no cost: "On the house". He told me to be careful with it and let him know if I liked it. I asked him what drug he gave me, but he just laughed and drove away.

I went up to my room and opened the envelope. There was $400 cash, and 3 tiny glassine envelopes that were labeled "MAC-10" with an image of a Mac 10 machine gun. Inside these tiny glassine envelopes was a brown powder; it was heroin. I had never seen heroin before. I heard that some kids in Suffern were starting to use it, but that kind of talk was taboo to me. Who uses heroin? Not me. Heroin is for junkies and scumbags, and that wasn't me. Well, if only junkies and scumbags used heroin, then I was one of them on that hot summer day in 2007. At the age of 19, I snorted my first bag of heroin. I was high for the entire day. When I called Pete and asked him where he got it, he replied, "Paterson, New Jersey." He said it was a 20-minute drive from Suffern. I told him that I like OxyContin better, but want to be able to use heroin when I couldn't get OxyContin. I asked him how much he paid for the three bags. He told me that he bought two bundles (20 bags) for $150. I was in shock. That meant the one bag that kept me high all day only cost $7.50. I would soon find out that if I went down to Paterson myself, I could get it even cheaper.

I asked him if he could hook me up with his connect. He told me to just drive down to Governor Street in Paterson, and I would find what I was looking for. I thought he was kidding; but he wasn't. There are several spots in Paterson that are open-air drug markets. Dealers sell heroin on the corners in plain sight. When they see a white boy with New York plates roll up, the corner boys swarm your car like bees around a hive. The whole process usually involves several players.

The first time I drove down to Paterson I had no idea what to expect. I had Pete and another one of his friends in the car with me. Pete laughed as he said, "Make a right at the third light of fright." We made a right off of Broadway onto East 18th Street and I could not believe what I saw. There were young dealers flagging us down trying to get us to stop the car to sell us heroin. Pete told me to keep going until we got to the corner where his guy set up shop.

We pulled up to the corner of Governor and Carroll Street when Pete pointed out his dealer wearing a Dallas Cowboys Michael Irvin jersey, number 88. The dealer hopped in the back seat and told me to drive down Carroll Street.

He asked us how much we wanted. A few seconds later we got to the corner of Carroll and Fulton Street, and the dealer jumped out of the car quickly. He came back in an instant with a kid who couldn't have been more than 12 years old. The kid handed us our heroin and the dealer got back into the car. We gave him his money and he told me to drive up Fulton and loop around on Rosa Parks Boulevard. I made a right on Rosa Parks Boulevard and the dealer pointed to the corner of Governor Street. He opened the door as the car was still moving and vanished into the alley. The deal was done.

Pete directed me out onto Broadway and to the bridge that crosses over the Passaic River. As soon as we got over the bridge, he told me to hold my breath. The next mile or so until we got off Route 4 back onto the Garden State Parkway is where everyone gets nailed by Elmwood Park Police. The Elmwood Park Police wait for addicts to leave the dope spots and pull them over on Broadway. We made it onto the Garden State Parkway and we all let out a sigh of relief. I successfully completed my first heroin buy.

I had no idea what I was getting myself into when Pete asked me if I wanted to go down to Paterson to cop dope. The experience was exhilarating, mind blowing, and exhausting. I went down with him one more time the following week and then decided it was too risky to continue. My OxyContin supply was fairly consistent, so I didn't need to take on an additional risk. My OxyContin deals were made in my own neighborhood: "the cobblestone jungle." A drug deal was the last thing anyone expected in my neighborhood.

I went back to work part-time at the mortgage bank in the summer. My opioid addiction was worse than before my four-wheeling accident. In June of 2007, I was waiting outside for my friend "C" to pick me up. He was the one who took my $10,000 when I was a senior to buy 5 pounds of weed and claimed he was robbed by his dealer. A few months earlier it came to my knowledge that he was not robbed; I was. He took part in taking my money and made up the robbery story. He came clean with me about it and started paying me back.

One night, "C" was on the way to my house late at night and said he was leaving a party and wanted to come get high and watch *The Wire*. He told me he would be at my house in 15 minutes. I was waiting outside smoking a cigarette, leaning on one of my crutches. I was down to one crutch at this point. About 15 minutes went by, no "C"; 20 minutes turned into 30 and still no "C.". Finally, I called him, but there was no answer. After about 45 minutes I called him one more time. He didn't answer, so I called it quits for the night. I went downstairs in the basement and passed out watching *The Wire.*

The next morning my mom came downstairs in a panic. She received a phone call early that morning from a close friend telling her that my friend died in a terrible car accident. He died on the way to my house, and I was the last person to talk to him.

The death of my friend messed me up for a while. Knowing that I was the last person to speak to him and that he died in a car accident on the way to my house was truly devastating. I couldn't believe I was angry when he never showed up and realized that he would never show up again.

I talked to his younger sister after his death. We talked about all the crazy things he and I did together, and how I could end up in the same situation if I didn't get my act together. This should have been enough to scare me straight, but it wasn't. If anything, my addiction became even worse after his death.

On September 7, 2007, all of my connections for OxyContin were dry. I called Pete to see if he would go down to Paterson for me if I bought him a few bags. He said that he was no longer using heroin or painkillers and was taking a medication called Suboxone to help keep him off opioids. I had never heard of Suboxone before. He said it was similar to Methadone, which is a drug that is used as an alternative to heroin. Suboxone is supposed to help with cravings and block the pleasurable effects of any opioid. That means if you try to use heroin or painkillers while taking Suboxone, you will not get high.

Since he was trying to get clean and I could not get any OxyContin, my disease convinced me that I had no choice but to go down to Paterson to buy heroin. I was in my backyard ripping shots with my lacrosse stick at the goal deciding if I was going to take the risk of going down to P-town to cop dope. After a few minutes of going back and forth in my head, I decided to go. I knew I couldn't drive in my silver Acura RSX with chrome rims. I would either get arrested by the police or robbed by the dealers. I have a friend who drove down to Paterson to buy heroin in his father's Lexus at night. The trip did not go as planned. Someone stuck a gun in his face, beat the hell out of him, took his money, stole his dad's car, and left him in the streets of Paterson.

In an effort to avoid detection, I stayed in my work clothes from my day at the mortgage bank and drove Nana's 1996 gold Toyota Camry with a handicapped license plate. I thought it was a brilliant move. I had driven down to Governor Street to buy heroin twice before, so I knew where I was going. I was nervous during the entire ride. Once I made the right turn at the third light of fright off Broadway onto East 18th Street, I knew it was game time.

Pete got the cell phone number of his dealer and called him ahead of time to give him the description of the car I would be driving and to let him know that I would be arriving around 6:15. He told me his dealer would be wearing a white t-shirt and a Pittsburgh Pirates baseball hat. I saw him instantly and he signaled me to pull over. He came up to the window and asked me what I wanted. I said, "give me a bun," which was 10 bags of heroin. He said "$70, wait here, I'll be right back." He disappeared into an abandoned house for a few minutes and came back to my car window. The first two times I drove down the dealer got in the car. This time we just did a hand to hand exchange on the block.

The dealers don't stick around after they make the deal. As I pulled away, I looked in my rearview mirror and he was gone. I made a left on Carroll Street and headed back towards Broadway. I turned onto Broadway and started driving towards the Garden State Parkway. My eyes were going back and forth between the road ahead of me and, more importantly, the road behind me. Pete told me to keep an eye out for unmarked police vehicles because they would be the ones to pull me over.

This begs the question, "If it's an unmarked police car, how do you even know it's a police car?" The answer is, we just know. I crossed over the bridge above the Passaic River and my heart was beating out of my chest. Just as I thought I was in the clear, a blacked-out Ford Crown Victoria appeared in my rearview mirror. I stayed calm at first, hoping they were just on regular patrol. There was a one car buffer between us, but then the car behind me merged into the next lane. Now the unmarked police car was on my tail. I could see the blue and red lights deep in the grille of the front end of the vehicle. I tried to merge into the next lane as the other car did, but I was so nervous that I almost hit another car. The red and blue lights went on instantly. I was being pulled over by Elmwood Park Police leaving the dope spot, ridin dirty.

I was unable to eat the heroin as I had done so many times when I was pulled over with a small amount of marijuana; that would be a death sentence. Pete told me to shove the heroin in my body cavity if I was pulled over. That would be my only chance of getting away without getting arrested. So, I did just that. I got the heroin down my pants as I pulled over to the side of the road.

I looked in the rearview mirror and one plainclothes officer got out of the car. This guy was about 6 feet 4 inches and jacked up! He had spiked hair with frosted tips, wore ripped jeans with black boots, and had on a black t-shirt. I knew this wasn't going to go well.

He came up to my window and asked me for my license, registration, and proof of insurance. Before I could even hand it to him he asked, "Do you want to tell me why you are down here?" My excuse was going to be that I was meeting a client for work and was lost, but I barely even got a word out before the plainclothes officer said in an aggressive tone, "Just stop. Don't waste my time and I won't waste yours. I know you have dope in the car, so just hand it over. I will write you a summons, and you can be on your way."

Of course, I denied having any drugs in the car. The cop said, "Get the fuck out of the car." As I opened my door and stepped out of the car, another unmarked police vehicle and marked patrol car pulled up with their lights flashing. Now there were three officers on the scene.

The patrolmen in uniform began searching Nana's Camry, which I had taken without her permission. Nana did not have an updated insurance card in the car, and the officers immediately used that against me. They told me I could not drive the car home without one. They let me make a phone call to my mother to ask her where the insurance card might be in Nana's car. My mom answered the phone and I told her I was pulled over in Nana's car and I could not find her insurance card.

My mother immediately began hammering me with questions, "Why do you have Nana's car and not your car? Why did you take Nana's car without asking? Why did you get pulled over? Where are you? Do you have drugs in the car?" The officers got frustrated and made me hang up the phone. My mother tried calling back several times in a panic, but I could not answer.

The big, aggressive officer that originally pulled me over began searching me. The third officer was also in plain clothes. He was the nice guy in the "good cop bad cop" routine. He began asking me questions and telling me how they were just doing their job and actually trying to help me. The officer told me that they do this all day long. He started asking me if I had ever gone for treatment or to support groups before.

I was hesitant to talk to him. I told him I became addicted to painkillers in a four-wheeling accident. I admitted that I was down there to buy heroin, but said I couldn't find any. They all laughed and one of the officers said, "On a Friday night it's harder to not find heroin in this area." The aggressive officer asked, "So you didn't pull up on Governor Street and buy dope off the kid wearing the white t-shirt and black baseball hat?" I was shocked by his remarks.

The "good cop" just shrugged his shoulders and said, "Listen buddy, we didn't pull you over for no reason. We saw you buy off that guy, and we followed you off the block." They had searched me twice already, and didn't find the heroin down my pants. Then, the "bad cop" asked to see my license again. He looked at it and said, "Oh, you're from Suffern. The dope must be up his ass. What is it with you guys from Suffern, you all like to drive around with dope up your ass?" He proceeded to tell me that I was the sixth person from Suffern that they arrested that day and that five out of the six had the dope down their pants and up their asses.

They threatened to arrest me for Loitering to Obtain or Distribute a Controlled Dangerous Substance. I had never heard of this charge before, and I became very agitated. They said they had to bring me down to the station for questioning and were going to have the K-9 Unit search me. The "good cop" told me if I walked into a police station with heroin down my pants the criminal charge would become a felony. I thought for a few minutes about what I should do. I finally gave in. I reached down the back of my pants and pulled out the ten bags of heroin bundled together by a rubber band.

The "bad cop" gladly slapped the handcuffs on me tightly and tossed me in the back of the patrol car. I was charged with Careless Driving and Possession of a Controlled Dangerous Substance in a Motor Vehicle.

The cops brought me down to the station to be processed. Two detectives came into the room where I was being fingerprinted and asked me if I wanted anything to eat or drink. They brought me a cup of water and told the officers to bring me into their office once they were done processing me.

The two plainclothes officers and one detective sat down and talked to me for a few minutes. They told me about the spike in heroin addiction going on in the area and that I needed to get help. The detective stated matter of factly, "That stuff will either kill you or ruin your life. You're only 19 years old and you have your entire life ahead of you. Cut the shit now before it's too late."

Nana's car was impounded, so I couldn't drive home. Also, the cops had to bring me to the hospital because I had shoved heroin inside of my body. If one of the bags would have ripped open, I could have easily overdosed and died. I refused medical assistance when I got to the hospital. I signed myself out against medical advice, and the cops dropped me off at a nearby Walmart. Before I got out of the car they warned me not to go back to buy more heroin. The cops said they couldn't believe how many times they would arrest people, release them, and then they would go back into the hood and try buying dope again.

I had my friends, Scott and Walter, pick me up in the Walmart parking lot. When my friends came and picked me up, they were shocked that I was in such a bad neighborhood alone. Walter asked, "Do I even want to know why you are down here and where your car is?" Neither of them messed around with drugs the way I did. I just told them the less they know the better.

I finally called my mother back and she picked up after the first ring. I told her I was okay but that the cops impounded Nana's car because she did not have a current insurance card in the car. My mother did not believe me, and kept asking if I got arrested. I lied, and told her, "The cops were just harassing me like they always do."

I forgot to take the hospital band off of my wrist that the nurse gave me when the cops brought me to the hospital. As soon as I walked in the house, my mother noticed it right away. She started screaming at me, "Why were you in the hospital? What the fuck is going on?" I had no choice but to come clean about what had happened. When I showed my parents the arrest report and they saw the word "heroin," they were shocked. Today, when anyone in my family hears of a heroin overdose, it does not shock us at all.

I was arrested four times between the ages of 18 and 19. The three previous arrests in New York gave me an ACD (Adjournment in Contemplation of Dismissal). My charges in New York were dismissed and sealed. My arrest in Elmwood Park would be my first in New Jersey. The court put me in a PTI (Pre-Trial Intervention Program). I was put on probation for six months and had to report to a probation officer. As long as I abided by the conditions set forth by my probation and was not rearrested within those six months, the charges against me would be dismissed.

I received a notice in the mail that I had to report to the Bergen County Department of Probation. I went there thinking that I would just have to sign some paperwork and would then be on my way. The probation officer handed me a drug test and told me I needed to give her a urine sample. I panicked. I knew coming clean was the best approach, so I told her I had no idea I was being drug tested and never stopped using since my arrest.

She was actually pretty understanding. She told me I needed to enroll in an outpatient program, so I called my former counselor, Joseph Lanzone. I had to see Joseph once a week and submit to random drug tests. I had not seen him in a few years. He was very concerned to hear that I was arrested with heroin in my possession.

I stopped smoking weed immediately, but could not wrap my addicted brain around giving up the opioids. My dad had purchased a few drug tests from Joseph when I saw him a few years earlier. He was still using the same tests. Marijuana stays in your system for a long time, but opioids do not. If I drank enough water, I figured out that I could test clean if I stopped using just 23 hours before my drug test. To play it safe, I would go for a day and a half without using.

A few weeks into our weekly meetings, Joe had to postpone our session due to an emergency with another one of his clients. He told me I had to come in the following day to see him since I was court mandated. I had stopped using for 36 hours at this point. I was so pissed off because I had to wait another 24 hours before I could use OxyContin again.

I was lying in bed watching a movie when my mind started to race and I felt physically ill. My joints hurt, and I had a headache and the chills. I was with a friend of mine and told him I thought I had the flu. He was sitting at my computer, and said to me, "You don't have the flu bro, you're dope sick." I knew that people who were addicted to opioids went through withdrawals when they stopped using, but I had never really experienced withdrawals before that night. I felt sick when I stopped taking the pain killers that were prescribed to me after I broke my leg, but it was nothing like this feeling. My friend typed OxyContin withdrawal symptoms into Google and started reading them. My symptoms were a match, but I still wasn't sure if I was really going through withdrawals, (dope sick), or if I had the flu or a virus.

The answer to my question would come the next morning. I scheduled my appointment as early as possible so I could start using OxyContin again right after my drug test. I went into see Joseph, and of course, he didn't even test me that day. I ran out of his office after our session ended and rushed home. There was a cop behind me the last time I left Joseph's office, so I stopped bringing the drugs in the car with me. As soon as I got home, I rushed upstairs and started crushing up an 80mg Oxy. I broke it up into 4 lines and immediately banged up 2 of them. Within minutes, all the sick-like symptoms were gone. I knew then that I was physically dependent on and addicted to opioids. There is no better high than going from dope sick to euphoria in a matter of minutes, sometimes even seconds.

I made a lot of money selling weed while I was on probation because I wasn't smoking. I sold enough OxyContin so I could use for free, but never really turned a profit. I managed to make it through probation without a violation. My 6 months was up and things went back to normal in April of 2008. "Normal" for me is smoking 10 blunts a day, snorting lines of OxyContin, and selling large quantities of marijuana. As if my lifestyle were not a gamble already, I decided to roll the dice just a little bit more.

CHAPTER 23
Falling into the Abyss

In June of 2008 one of my close friends, Kris, turned 21 years old. We call him KP. He was the leader of my core group of friends from high school. For his 21st birthday, we all piled into a super stretch limo and headed down to Atlantic City. We were smoking, drinking, and blasting music all the way down the Garden State Parkway. Most of my friends had already turned 21, but some of us were still only 20, including me. You have to be 21 years old to be on the casino floor let alone gamble. Our hotel did not have a casino, but we went over to Harrah's Resort & Casino after dinner. I had borrowed a friend's driver's license to get in.

I had only gambled once before on a vacation in Puerto Rico. Once we arrived at Harrah's, we started off at the roulette table. I wasn't even carded. It seemed as if each of us was winning. We would pick a color and would throw down our chips together so we could celebrate as a team. We had a lot of fun. I was told to stay away from table games because the pit bosses would definitely ID me as soon as I sat down, and the ID I had really didn't look that much like me.

We all got wasted and decided it was time to try to get into a nightclub. Everyone who had a fake ID or was using someone else's was denied at the door. I ended up taking a cab back to our hotel. I was the only one staying in my hotel room who was denied, so I just went back to my room and ripped lines of Oxy and smoked cigarettes. At this point, none of my friends in that group abused opioids, so I kept it a secret from them as long as I could. As time went on, some of them would fall into the same bad drug habits as I did.

It was around the same time as KP's 21st birthday extravaganza that I received a call from one of my friends, Sean, asking about prices for pounds of high grade marijuana. He told me he had a friend who lived in Edison, New Jersey who had lost his connection and needed a new one. He said he needed about 2 pounds a week. I was hesitant to meet this guy because I did not know who he was. I told Sean I would give him a free sample to show his friend. If he liked it, he could send Sean over with the money. I was not willing to sell 2 pounds of marijuana to someone I did not know.

Sean came by and got the sample. About 30 minutes later, I got the call from him informing me that his friend wanted 2 pounds, but that he had to see the product before he handed over the cash. I told Sean this wouldn't work for me and hung up the phone. Of course, they called right back. When I answered, it wasn't Sean, it was his friend who wanted the weed. His name was Greenberg. We talked on the phone for a few minutes and he tried to convince me to let him come to my house with Sean. Sean vouched for him and said it was cool, so I decided to let my guard down and let him come to my house. It was well past midnight.

They came up to my room where I was watching a movie with my friend Brendan. Sean introduced me to Greenberg and we started talking. He told me he wanted 2 pounds, so I went into my basement into the back room where I kept my stuff. I called this room "Crack." It was a back storage room that was the only unfinished part of the basement at my parents' house. We had a card table, couches, and sound system. A lot of bad things went on in that back room in the late hours of the night. It wasn't the same feeling as the late night's smoking weed in high school while listening to Phish in a room with black lights and glow-in-the-dark posters. It was a much dirtier and darker feel. Crack was a scary place to be.

I came back to my room and handed Greenberg the 2 pounds of high quality weed. I charged him $10,800, which was a $1,200 profit for me. Before he left, he said, "Do you mind if I do a few lines here before I head out?" I assumed he meant cocaine. I replied, "Knock yourself out." He opened up a backpack he was carrying and pulled out a large orange pill bottle. The label was ripped off so you could see right through it. It was filled to the top with round green pills. I asked, "Are those 80's?" He said, "Yeah man, I have a crazy OxyContin supply. Sean didn't tell me you messed around with that stuff." I told Greenberg to take a seat, we had a lot of business to discuss.

It was the summer of 2008 and OxyContin abuse was steadily on the rise. The range in the price for an 80mg OxyContin during that time was astronomical. I got them for as low as $30 to as high as $80 a pill. At the time I met Greenberg, I was paying $40 a pill. I had a decent supply before I met him. I was able to maintain my addiction and sell just enough so I could use for free. There were never any extras. Often times, I would use too much and have to dip into my pocket or buy from another source at a significantly higher price, but Greenberg was about to solve my problems.

He said he could get me as much as I wanted. We made an arrangement where every two weeks we would trade 2 pounds of weed for 325 80mg OxyContin pills. They were never the generic version. These were the real circular green pills with OC on the front and 80 on the back. I called them the "Green Monsters." I was skeptical about him actually following through on what he promised. How in the hell could anyone get their hands on that many OxyContin? Sure enough, 2 weeks later I got the call. I lied to him and said that my license was suspended in New Jersey, so he had to drive to my house in New York. This way I never had to drive with the drugs in my car and risk getting pulled over.

He came to my house and took out 325 OC 80's in a vacuum sealed bag. I was shocked, and I don't get shocked easily. I handed him the 2 pounds of weed as promised. Over the next seven months, we barely paid cash for any of our transactions. I always paid in marijuana, and he paid in OxyContin. It was a mutually beneficial relationship in my addicted brain, but a mutually detrimental relationship in reality. My addiction to OxyContin progressed quickly once I started dealing with Greenberg. Since I never had to worry about running out, I started using more. I went from 2 or 3 80's a day to 10-12 80's a day over the course of a few months.

I got involved with drugs when I was only 14 years old. It soon became more than a habit; it became a dependent lifestyle. I started using and selling drugs for all of the classic peer pressure reasons. I wanted to be cool, popular, fit in, and be accepted. The list goes on and on. How did I go from selling half ounces of weed and smoking a few times a day to selling pounds of weed and hundreds of pills of OxyContin? How did I progress to smoking a minimum of 10 blunts and snorting 10-12 80mg Oxys a day?

Addiction is a fatal progressive illness, and so is the lifestyle that goes with it. One day, I woke up and realized how far I had fallen. It wasn't about being cool or fitting in anymore; now it was about maintaining my addiction and hiding it from everyone. I never had any form of social media because I never wanted anyone to know where I was or what I was doing. I wanted my existence to be forgotten by anyone who was not involved in the mysterious drug underworld. It seemed like this would be my bottom. How could things get any worse? Every time I thought I had hit bottom, a trap door would open, and I would plunge deeper into the abyss.

CHAPTER 24
The Cruise to Nowhere

In August of 2008, my family went on a cruise with three other families. I wasn't going to turn 21 for another month, so I couldn't buy alcohol legally on the ship. That didn't stop me, but my focus was not on alcohol anyway. Luckily, the age for gambling at the casino on the ship was only 18.

I was a full-blown OxyContin addict by this time. How could I go on a family vacation without my lover and mistress? I could not survive without her. I was head over heels in love with OxyContin. I would be heartbroken without her. I remembered what the withdrawal symptoms were like from when I had a two pill a day habit. I had increased that tenfold by this point. My only option was to smuggle OxyContin onto the ship.

I knew I had to go through customs, so this was a very risky move. What person in his right mind would smuggle drugs into international waters? Clearly, I was not in my right mind at all. Even worse, I was going away for a full week, so I had to smuggle 84 pills in order to maintain my 12 pill a day habit. If I was caught with that amount, I would likely be charged with intent to distribute.

The night before we left I bought a bottle of Advil. Over the counter medications such as Advil have a seal that needs to be broken on the top. I took a razor blade and cut around the seal so it would come off without being ripped. I emptied the Advil and then filled the bottom with the 84 OxyContin I needed to bring with me. Then I put the Advil pills back in on top of the OxyContin. I took the seal that I had cut off and glued it back on. I put the top on the bottle, and then put the bottle back in the box. I glued the box shut and stuffed it into my luggage. I was good to go.

We were flying to Florida from JFK first, so I would have to go through two different checkpoints. I was much more concerned about bringing it on the cruise ship than the plane to Florida. A few of my friends told me that security officers do a thorough search of your bags on a cruise ship.

I went through security at JFK with ease. The pills were in my carry-on bag; there was no way I was putting them in with the bag I checked. If the bag were lost, I would go ballistic.

Once we arrived at the ship, we met up with the three other families. We walked up to the checkpoint together. I was trying to keep calm and look natural by acting excited and talking to all of the people in our party. My heart began to pound out of my chest as we approached the checkpoint. My dad was in front of me, and they searched his book bag. They said his sunglasses holder looked like it could be a weapon. I was next. I went through without a problem. I made it on the ship, went back to my room, and immediately broke out an Oxy for a celebration high.

I went downstairs the first night and started playing roulette. I was going back and forth all night until I finally lost the $300 cash I had with me. I loved to gamble and wanted more action.

As soon as I turned 21 years old, I was ready to hit the casinos in Atlantic City. A few weeks before my 21st birthday, the unthinkable happened. My OxyContin dealer went on vacation without telling me. I was doomed. I only had a day's supply left, and I knew I was in big trouble if I didn't find some quickly. I didn't panic right away because I had so many different connections and was confident I could buy enough to hold me over until he returned. For some reason, no matter who I called, the supply was dry. I debated whether or not I would buy heroin to hold me over, but decided that would have to be a last resort.

After 24 hours without Oxy, I started to feel sick. It wasn't anything unbearable at first. The mental obsession was far worse than the physical obsession at that point. I felt like I was going to die without my mistress. My mind was racing. I decided to take a Xanax to help me sleep. It worked, but I would wake up the next morning in full withdrawal. My sheets were soaking wet from sweating throughout the night. I had the chills, my head was pounding, and my joints ached with shooting pains. As soon as I got out of bed, the vomiting began.

Nana was the only one home that morning. She heard me throwing up and saw what I looked like. She told me that we had to go to the hospital. I thought the hospital would give me painkillers to help with the withdrawals; I was wrong. Not unlike the ATV crash, that was one of the worst days of my life. I didn't even know it was possible to feel that sick. That's what happens when you snort 960mgs of OxyContin a day for several months consistently and come to a screeching halt. It's like driving 100mph down the thruway and crashing into a brick wall.

I ended up in my first detox that night at Good Samaritan Hospital. The doctors gave me some medication to help with the withdrawal symptoms. Even though phones weren't allowed on the detox floor, I managed to smuggle my cell phone into the hospital. I felt much better the following morning, but was still feeling pretty awful. I got a call from my friend, Dan, telling me his connect just filled a prescription for 120 40mg OxyContin and would sell the entire bottle to me for a good price. I immediately signed out Against Medical Advice (AMA).

Dan picked me up in the hospital parking lot. We drove to my house, and I ran inside to get the cash. No one in my family saw me as I was in and out pretty quickly. We took a 3-minute drive down the street to Walgreens. The dealer already filled his prescription inside and was waiting for us in the parking lot. He came to the window and we did a quick hand to hand deal. I instantly took out a textbook from the back of Dan's car and started breaking up lines right in the parking lot. I gave Dan a few free pills for getting the Oxys for me. I snorted two 40mg pills at once, lit up a cigarette, and laid back in the front seat of Dan's G35 coupe.

Within seconds, I went from feeling sick to feeling dopamine rush throughout my entire body. This is what keeps addicts hooked. Knowing that when we are feeling our absolute worst we can get the feeling we crave and love in an instant. All the sickness slips away along with any stress or worries. The rapper, Lil Wayne, could not have said it better. In his song, *I Feel Like Dying*, his lyrics ring true: "Only once the drugs are done, I feel like dying."

I enrolled in classes at Rockland Community College (RCC) simply to show my parents a piece of paper saying I was attending school. This would keep them off my back for a short period of time. I would leave the house during the hours I was supposed to be in class to make my parents think I was actually attending classes. My 21st birthday finally arrived, and I decided to bring a new vice into my life full-force: gambling.

CHAPTER 25
The Gamble of a Lifetime

By the time I was 21 years old, I had saved over $100,000 selling marijuana. I sold OxyContin too, but that was only to support my habit. I was lucky to break even considering the large amount I was using. I wasn't the type to blow money on material things and I wasn't flashy either. I bought a gold chain for $2500, a watch for $750, and leased an Acura RSX. Other than that, I preferred to save my money and watch it grow. A lot of that had to do with my recognizing that it was likely the day would come where all of this would come crashing down and I would need that money to get me out of trouble. This would end up being a self-fulfilling prophecy that would be practically insurmountable.

My friend Ryan taught me how to play blackjack, and we started going to the casinos in Atlantic City. We would stay at either the Tropicana or Harrah's. I would bring about $10,000 cash each time. I also used the casinos to shrink my money. I would bring $10,000 in 20 dollar bills, buy in at the $100 minimum high rollers table, then cash out with $100 bills.

Ryan loved to gamble; I loved to win. There is a difference. Ryan would go to have a good time and enjoyed the excitement of placing high stakes bets. Of course, no one likes to lose; however, as usual, I took it to another level. I would start my nights at a $50 minimum blackjack table and would place the minimum bet. If I lost, I would throw down another $50. If I lost that one, I would throw down $100, then $200, then $400. I just kept doubling my bets until I finally won a hand and got even. This is a very risky strategy, but it does tilt the odds in your favor providing you have enough cash and the guts to keep pushing. I could lose 7 hands in a row, but I would get back to even as long as I won the 8th. That actually happened to me at the roulette table.

I put $100 on black and lost. I kept doubling my bets all the way up to $3,200, and lost again. I lost seven hands in a row at roulette just playing colors. I held onto black the entire time, but red kept popping up. After losing my 7th bet at $3,200, I was now down $6,400. Luckily, I brought more than $10,000 with me that night because I would need to put $6,400 down on the next bet in order to break even. If I lost, I would be down $12,800. Ouch!

I was with Ryan and two other friends, Chris and Walter. I handed the $6,400 to Walter and told him to put it down on black one more time. I couldn't even do it myself. Walter walked over and cashed in the $6,400 and told the dealer to put it all on black. The maximum bet was $5,000 at the table we were playing at, but the pit boss approved the extra $1,200. It was go time!

The dealer then picked up the ball and spun it around the roulette wheel. I don't think I took a breath the entire time the ball was rolling around the wheel. It felt like the ball was rolling in slow motion. I clenched my fists eagerly waiting. The wheel started to slow down and the dealer said, "No more bets." The ball hit the table and bounced around the numbers. There were several others playing who were rooting for me. Everyone was scared to put their money on red because they watched me lose 7 hands in a row and saw the amount I was risking. The ball landed and the dealer called out, "Black 15!" I let out a roar and fist pumped along with everyone else at the table. The other players were giving me high fives as I waited for the dealer to pay out. I grabbed my chips and ran towards the cashier. I called it quits for the night.

Casinos track your bets with a player's card that they give you the first time you place a bet. The more you gamble and the more money you risk, the higher your status. That is how you get complimentary hotel rooms, meals, and more. Ryan and I both gambled like this often. Before long, we had hosts who took care of all of our needs. I used to say, "They give me free rooms and complimentary meals, I love it." The truth is that nothing at a casino is free. They don't build these enormous palatial structures by losing money and giving things away for free. In the end, the house always wins and the gambler always loses; in more ways than one.

I loved going to Atlantic City to drink, use drugs, party, gamble, and hook up with girls. It was everything an addict could hope for. But the idea of playing against the odds (the house) did not sit right with me. A few months later, just before 2009, an opportunity presented itself. I was approached by two other guys about coming in as a partner and financial backer of an online gambling service for sports betting and online casino games. In other words, they were bookies. The two guys running this racquet had gotten too big and did not have the funds to back the bets they were taking. Even though the odds were in their favor and it was a guaranteed money maker, a high roller could have a lucky few weeks and clean out a bookie if he didn't have the money to pay out.

This is the reason why casinos never lose. The odds are in their favor, and they have the backing to keep taking the bets of winning gamblers long enough to turn them into losers. The more you gamble, the more likely the house will take you for everything you have...and then some.

I knew someone else who had an interest in providing a service like this, and he recently hit a big jackpot playing poker. I brought him in as a fourth partner and we worked out an arrangement to share our clients and the profits four ways.

We had a website which was based out of Costa Rica where gambling services are legal. We paid this company a weekly fee for managing our website. The fee was $25 a week per player. We paid the website via Western Union. We would use fake names and addresses on the Western Union slip, and be sure to switch up the location as often as we could. Our clients were given a username and password to access the website and place their bets. There weren't any electronic financial transactions for our clients. Everything was based on credit.

Until this point, everything we did was legal and above board. We paid a company in Costa Rica that hosted a gambling website to manage our clients. When our clients placed a bet, it was considered to be play money because they never deposited funds into an account or handed over any cash. Where this service became illegal is the day after a week of betting when the cash transactions inside the United States took place. We collected the money from the losers on Monday and paid out the winners on Friday. We had several sales agents working for us who brought in their own clients and received a percentage of their overall losses.

I had no idea what I was getting myself into when I became part of this racket. After website fees and commission to our agents, we each took home just over $4,000 the first week. I was blown away. We all went to Atlantic City on New Year's Eve to celebrate our new business venture. The new year would start off with a financial bang followed by zooming unmarked police cars with red and blue flashing lights and narcotics officers screaming, "Police, don't fucking move."

CHAPTER 26
High Maintenance

I got a call from Greenberg, my OxyContin dealer, telling me he wanted to meet up and do our usual trade of 325 OxyContin pills for 2 pounds of high grade marijuana. I decided to stop selling drugs once I got involved in the gambling and was also trying to get off the OxyContin by using Suboxone. I was unsuccessful at numerous attempts to get off the opioids. I told Greenberg I would pay for the OxyContin in cash but that I could not get him his 2 pounds of marijuana. He said this was unacceptable and that he would not sell me any OxyContin if I did not bring him the 2 pounds of marijuana. We went back and forth arguing for a while, but he knew I was a full-blown OxyContin addict and would eventually give in.

He also asked for a favor. He wanted to know if I could drive down to where he lived in Edison, New Jersey, to make the deal. He told me a few weeks earlier that his wife just gave birth to their baby and he had to stay home to help her. I knew he was telling the truth because I saw his pregnant wife a few times in the front seat of his car.

I only drove two times previously to meet him, and it was at the rest stop on the Garden State Parkway near exit 177. It was just over the border of New York into New Jersey, less than a ten-minute drive for me. He asked to meet at the Red Roof Inn in Edison. This was an hour drive for me. I never drove far with that much weight in the car. I tried to convince him to do our usual routine and have him come to my parents' house in New York, but he wasn't having it.

I was going to run out of OxyContin in a few days. There was no way I could let that happen, so I agreed. I paid one of my friends to follow me the entire way down to prevent any New Jersey State Police highway patrol cars from getting directly behind me. I took my dad's black Acura TL because I felt the chrome rims on my Acura RSX were too flashy to be riding with felony weight in the trunk.

I took I-287 the entire way with my friend on my tail. I saw numerous cars pulled over by New Jersey State Police on the side of I-287. I kept driving the speed limit, nice and smooth. I called Greenburg when my GPS said I was 10 minutes out. He told me to get off Exit 3 and make a right onto New Durham road, and the Red Roof Inn would be on my right. As I pulled up to the exit on I-287, I could see the Red Roof Inn from the thruway. My friend followed me off the exit, and we pulled into the parking lot of the hotel and parked next to each other. I had the 2 pounds of marijuana wrapped in a black garbage bag under the spare tire in the trunk. I walked up to my friend's window and told him he could head back to Suffern and meet me at my house.

Seconds later, unmarked cars came flying in from all angles with red and blue flashing lights. Greenberg set me up. Multiple narcotics officers in plain clothes jumped out of their vehicles. One in particular screamed "Police, don't fucking move!" They ran over fast and threw me up against the car. A few other officers ripped my friend out of the car and handcuffed him. They slapped the bracelets on me too.

The officer in charge introduced himself to me in a very polite manner. He told me that they knew I had 2 pounds of marijuana in the trunk and that they were also arresting Greenberg on the other side of the Red Roof Inn as we spoke. I knew that was a lie. Greenberg wasn't being arrested that night. That must have already happened and he cooperated with police and agreed to set me up in order to reduce his criminal charges.

The officer said, "If you are honest and respectful with us, I will do everything I can to help you." I responded, "Why don't you start by being honest with me and not lying about arresting Greenberg on the other side. I know he set me up." The officers laughed and smiled at each other, then they began searching my car. They searched the inside of my car and did not find anything. Then the police came up to me and asked if they could search my trunk. They told me if I didn't give them permission, they would bring down the K-9 Unit and the dog would hit on the trunk in a second.

Eventually, I told them the drugs were in the trunk. They popped open my dad's trunk and found the 2 pounds of marijuana. I told the officers that my friend had nothing to do with any of this and they agreed to let him go. I was not as lucky. A marked patrol car came and took me down to the station to be processed. Afterwards, the arresting officers read me my rights and began questioning me. I didn't answer any questions, but the damage was already done. They told me I was being charged with possession of marijuana with intent to distribute, an indictable offense which, in the state of New Jersey, is equivalent to a felony.

The officers said I would definitely end up going to jail if I didn't set someone else up. I asked to speak to an attorney and the questioning stopped. One of the officers said, "I wouldn't be able to sleep tonight knowing you were in the Middlesex County Jail; it's bad in there. We are going to release you on your own recognizance, just call someone to pick you up."

I tried calling my friend to come back, but he was terrified and refused to get me. There was no way I was calling my parents, so I called my Uncle Rich (Cook) to come pick me up. He came right away and arrived at the Edison Police Department in a little over an hour. The officers explained what was going on and what I was being charged with, and then they let me go.

Although I expected him to, Cook didn't lecture me on the ride home. He expressed his concern for me and asked if I realized how serious the consequences could be for my arrest. I was in my own world and still thought I was untouchable. I slept at his house that night and began researching criminal defense attorneys who practiced drug arrests regularly in that area. We came across an attorney named Mark Cheshire. I remember his website boasting the slogan, "From marijuana to murder, we defend it all."

I hired him as my attorney after speaking with him on the phone from the hospital. I ended up in the emergency room the night after my arrest because I was throwing up violently from OxyContin withdrawals. He told me I didn't have to go to my first court appearance and that he would represent me and let me know my next court date. About a month later, I walked into the Middlesex County, New Jersey Courthouse and found Mark. He introduced himself and brought me into a conference room. He casually said, "Right now the prosecutor is offering 365 days in the county jail, but let's see if we can work on that." My heart dropped to the floor as I finally comprehended what he was saying. I started to panic. My criminal defense attorney at home, David Goldstein, never said anything like that to me before. This was totally different because this was the first time I was being criminally charged at the felony level.

I thought to myself, "How did I get here?" I started to look back on the decisions I made that led me to be standing in a courtroom facing real jail time. It was surreal. Since I lost my OxyContin connect, I decided I was going to give the Suboxone maintenance program a try. I saw a doctor and was prescribed the maximum dosage, 24 mgs a day.

The Suboxone maintenance program is a controversial issue in recovery communities and amongst addiction specialists. The idea behind Suboxone is similar to Methadone. It is an alternative to abusing painkillers and/or heroin (opioids.) Suboxone helps with cravings and withdrawal symptoms and also serves as an opioid blocker, preventing someone from feeling the euphoric effects of taking a drug such as heroin or OxyContin. Suboxone is still a controlled substance, and in my experience, was actually harder to come off of than both heroin and OxyContin.

I was on and off Suboxone for over a year. Some people say that you aren't really sober if you are on Suboxone. I am not going to debate that issue, but I will say that in my experience, Suboxone should usually only be used for a short period of time. Many treatment programs do not allow you to take Suboxone even if it is prescribed by a doctor. I agree with this approach. Suboxone is a great drug to help opioid abusers detox by minimizing cravings and withdrawal symptoms. In my opinion, in most cases Suboxone should not be used for more than 7-10 days. If someone cannot refrain from abusing opioids without Suboxone, then he or she should be in a long-term treatment program. However, there are situations where a person has been through treatment several times and just keeps on failing, or cannot get into a long-term treatment program. A chronic relapser may need to be on Suboxone for a long period of time just to prevent them from using heroin or Oxy. This is referred to as the harm reduction approach.

Suboxone was a short-lived solution for me. I went to Lincoln Tech in Mahwah, New Jersey for barely a month before I dropped out. Tech school definitely wasn't for me. In fact, with the condition that I was in at that time, no school was for me. In that month, I found a new OxyContin dealer. History repeated itself, and the vicious cycle continued.

After a few court dates, which consisted of simply going through the legal motions that accompany my type of case, the prosecutor offered me a better plea deal. The offer was to plead guilty to possession with intent to distribute marijuana and receive 2 years probation. If I plead guilty to that charge, I would be convicted of an indictable offense, which is equal to a felony. I met with my attorney after the court appearance and he brought up another option. He told me that he had been looking over the case file and found some serious holes in the police report.

The entire case was based on the testimony of a confidential informant. The way the arresting officer worded the police report prompted my attorney to believe that the confidential informant was acting as an agent of the police, which can be grounds for the affirmative defense of entrapment. My attorney said he wanted to file 2 motions. The first was to release the identity of the confidential informant. If the judge approved the motion and the prosecution refused to release the identity of the informant, then my case will be dismissed and all of the charges against me would be dropped.

If the prosecution did release the identity of the informant, then my attorney would go with the entrapment defense and call the confidential informant to the stand to be questioned. I did not understand fully what was going on at the time, but my dad is an attorney and agreed with Mark Cheshire, and we decided to go to a motions hearing.

The morning of the motions hearing I was lit on OxyContin. I was so nervous I needed to take extra pills to calm me down. My eyes would get bloodshot red and my face pale as a ghost when I was high on OxyContin, which seemed to be all the time now. I used a lot of Visine that morning and used a little bit of my mom's bronzer to give my face some color. I wore a suit and was sure to shave my face that morning to make myself appear younger. The way I presented myself in the courtroom that morning, no one would think I was a drug addict or drug dealer, even though I was both.

I had many court appearances before that day, but those paled in comparison to this appearance. There were no other defendants in the courtroom, just me and all the players that make up the courtroom work group. My dad was the only spectator. My attorney gave me a pre-game pep talk before I walked in. He told me to be quiet, sit up straight, and pray that this would work. Since I turned down the deal the prosecutor offered, I could end up facing jail time if we lost the motions hearings. This was just another gamble for me. My attorney said depending on how things went with the prosecution's first witness, the arresting officer, I might have to take the stand and testify.

We walked into the courtroom as the judge emerged from his chambers. There were several Middlesex County Sheriffs in attendance. I felt like they were just waiting to slap the cuffs on me and take me to jail, and they were.

The motions hearing began with the prosecutor questioning the arresting officer. The prosecutor asked the officer some basic questions and details about the night in question. Then my attorney got up and cross examined the officer. I don't remember much of what transpired that day, I felt as if I were watching an episode of Law & Order. All I remember is that my attorney was poking holes in the officer's story and ripping apart just about everything the officer said. It was obvious that things were going in my favor. The officer's face was beat red as my attorney ripped into him. Mark Cheshire showed up ready to do battle that day. When he was done questioning the officer, he looked at the judge and said, "No more questions," and the prosecutor asked the judge for a short recess.

Mark sat down next to me and called my dad over to the defendant's table. He told us the prosecutor was going to come back in a few minutes with a plea offer that was better than the one before. He said, "He knows he is about to lose." He then told us that depending on the offer, I should consider taking the deal so I did not have to take the stand. Just as he predicted, the prosecutor came back in and called Mark over.

Mark talked with the prosecutor for less than a minute and came back and told me the offer. I was asked to plead guilty to simple possession of less than 50 grams of marijuana, which is a disorderly persons offense in New Jersey and equal to a misdemeanor. I would also have to be put on probation for two years. I knew probation meant I would have to report to a probation officer, submit to drug tests, and have to enter a treatment program. There was no way my disease was going to allow that to happen. I told Mark I would take the deal if there was no probation. He went back and talked to the prosecutor, and I heard the prosecutor respond in an angry and frustrated tone: "Fine, whatever." Mark came back with a big smile on his face. He earned every penny of his fee that day.

The judge came back from his chambers and accepted the plea offer. He gave me a stern talking to before he dismissed me. He let me know that I "dodged a big bullet today," and should be thanking my attorney for the performance he put on. The judge said, "I wouldn't even jaywalk on your way out of this courthouse if I were you." One of the last things the judge said to me was how he could tell that I was sober and hoped I was getting treatment for my substance abuse. I addressed the court and told the judge I was going to NA meetings and was sober for a few months. He congratulated me on my sobriety without realizing that I lied right to his face. Little did he know I was blasted on OxyContin while standing in his courtroom. I actually went into the bathroom and snorted a few bumps of Oxy during the recess.

I went over to the clerk's office to pay my fine and walked out of the courthouse a free man. My dad and I had a long talk on the way home. He said he couldn't believe it was his son sitting in the defendant's chair during that hearing. He was hoping this close call would scare me straight and I would start to turn things around. There really was nothing that could scare me straight. There were many times throughout my addiction when I wanted to stop living the stress-filled insane lifestyle which was my reality, but OxyContin had me in her grips and refused to let go. No matter how hard I tried, I couldn't kick the habit. Since I couldn't beat my addiction, I had no choice but to commit illegal acts to maintain my habit. It truly was out of my control.

CHAPTER 27
California Dreaming

After my close call with the criminal justice system in the spring of 2009, things started to get bad at home. My parents knew I was a drug addict, a drug dealer, a gambler, and a bookie. They knew I was still taking enormous risks and destroying the Hill name. They kept hoping I would snap out of it. Maybe all of this was just a phase. They were waiting for me to turn my life around, but it was not happening. Things just kept on going from bad to worse, and they couldn't take it anymore. Something had to change.

Some of our family friends and other people in the community maligned my parents as if my addiction and criminal behavior was their fault. We even had family members judging me and my parents. Friends and family would give my parents advice on what they should do with me. "Kick him out; cut him off; have him arrested." These were just a few of the phrases used. Most of these people had absolutely no experience dealing with a child suffering from substance abuse and were speaking to my parents as if they were professionals working in the field of addiction.

My dad kicked me out several times over the years when I was abusing drugs. I would stay with a friend or family member for a few days and then come back home when I knew he wasn't around. It's usually much harder for a mother to kick her child out of the house than it is for the father, and my mom was no exception. One argument my mom would give my father was that I was not like most drug addicts because I had so much money. She believed the power of kicking a kid out of the house comes with having no money and nowhere to stay. That wouldn't be a problem for me.

In November of 2009, my dad was about to kick me out again, but I just blurted out, "I'll go to treatment." This would be the first time I went to treatment on my own, without my parents forcing me into it. I also did not have any criminal charges pending at the time and was not on any kind of probation. I was free to do what I wanted. I saved a lot of money gambling, so I decided to spend some of it on treatment. Once again, my desperate mother searched high and low looking for the best treatment facility in the country. She found a place in Newport Beach, California called Sober Living By The Sea. It was reputed to be a top of the line facility. My mother picked this place because not only was it a top ranked facility, but its location on the beach and the fun sober activities that were part of the program would give me the best shot at learning to live a happy and healthy life in recovery. I lived in a beautiful house right on Newport Beach. This was not your usual inpatient treatment facility. We participated in a lot of activities outside the house. I actually had a great time throughout my stay there.

I was only at that facility for 30 days before I went back to New York. I went home just before Christmas and stayed there until just after New Year's. A family friend of my Uncle Dave had a sober house in Oceanside, California where I was going to stay. I decided to move out there and enroll in the local community college.

CHAPTER 28
The Not So Sober House

I moved into the Tropicana Sober House in early January of 2010 before the spring semester began. I did not know a single person. I became friendly with some of the younger guys who were living in the sober house. As it turned out, the house was not so sober. More than half the guys in the house were still using drugs and alcohol. There was a house manager living there, but he worked during the days. There really was not much oversight at all.

I was on Suboxone the entire time I was living in the "sober" house. I only lasted about 2 months before I started drinking alcohol and smoking pot again. I did not have a job because I had saved up a lot of money and felt working for minimum wage was beneath me. Remember, "The working man is a sucker." I ended up dropping 4 out of my 5 classes in a matter of weeks. The only class I did not drop was a marketing class. I was interested in this class because the majority of your final grade was based on a semester long marketing project of a business of your choice. Of course, I chose legal online gambling. I got an A in that class and based on my experience, I could have been the instructor.

I went home for spring break in late March of 2010 for a week. I saw a bunch of my friends and told them I would be moving back to New York in May once my semester ended. I went back to California on April 4, 2010. Just 3 days later I got a call from Conor. He had terrible news. One of our best friends, Walter, suddenly died from spinal meningitis. I can remember vividly lying on the couch when I answered the phone and how I jumped up when I heard the horrific news. I cried my eyes out that night. I couldn't believe he was gone. He was at my house the day I left to go back to California, and he was perfectly fine.

I took a flight home that day to pay my respects to Walter's family and to be with my friends. We were all very torn up about his death. I didn't even want to go back to California to finish the one class I was taking, but I did. When I came home for Walter's funeral, I reconnected with a girl I was seeing on and off over the past few years. We started dating when I returned to New York in mid May of 2010. I promised her that I would stay sober, go back to school, and not be involved in drugs.

A week before I came home, an idea popped into my head while I was watching the movie *Blow*. I was drunk and high sitting on the couch in my not so sober house, when I saw Johnny Depp playing the real life drug dealer, George Jung. Jung was smuggling marijuana from California to the east coast because the quality was significantly better and the prices were significantly cheaper. This was still true in 2010.

My roommate at the time, Anthony, told me some months earlier that his friend was a grower. I was not sure if I believed him or not. Either way, even if he did know a grower, I did not think it was on any kind of large scale. Since I had a ton of cash lying around, I thought I would at least try to score some California marijuana and send it back to New York to sell for a hefty profit. I shipped my car out to California from New York on a car carrier trailer. My plan was to send my car back to New York loaded with high quality California marijuana. First, I had to see if I could get my hands on what I was looking for. I asked Anthony about his connect and he said he would give him a call. The next day we had a meeting at a bar owned by one of his friends.

Anthony and I went to the bar and met the grower directly. He brought a few samples with him and told me the prices per pound. I was blown away at the quality and significantly cheaper prices as compared to the east coast. I was nervous to ask for the amount I wanted, but I did it anyway. I ended up buying 10 pounds of high grade marijuana for $27,000. Back home in New York, I could easily double my money.

The grower told me my plan to ship the marijuana across the country in my car on a car carrier trailer was not a good one. He believed that was too risky because of weigh stations and checkpoints. He suggested I vacuum seal the 10 pounds, wrap them in dryer sheets to get rid of the smell, stuff them in a large dog food container, and ship it in the mail across the country.

The day before I moved back to New York, I shipped my 10 pounds of weed in the mail overnight. I still get anxiety when I recall how nervous and stressed I was for those 24 hours. What kind of person would take such an enormous risk? Who in their right mind would even consider such behavior? Yet again, I was not in my right mind. I put a fake name on the box and shipped it to my friend's house. On schedule, I got the call 24 hours later informing me that the package arrived safely.

A week before I moved back to New York I had every intention of staying sober, going back to school, and not getting involved in illegal activities. I made a promise to my girlfriend, a promise I intended on keeping; at least that was my intention.

My girlfriend picked me up at the airport, and within a few hours of being home, I picked up my 10 pounds of marijuana and sent $500 overseas to Costa Rica to restart my gambling business.

How does that happen so quickly? Why was my brain so susceptible to such risky behavior? Being under the influence of drugs for so long and starting at such an early age made my brain a sponge for negativity. I was drawn to the criminal underworld that is so glorified in rap songs, television shows, and movies. I got involved in all of this at the early age of 14 because I wanted to be cool. Now it became a part of who I was, and it was getting increasingly serious with each passing day. Drugs became my identity. I used to be Stephen Hill the hockey player, or the lacrosse player. Now it became Stephen Hill the drug addict, the drug dealer.

CHAPTER 29
Threading the Needle

Upon my return from California, I managed to not use drugs or alcohol for the first few weeks. I wasn't even smoking even though I was selling the weed I brought home from California. I was still taking Suboxone, and had been for over 6 months. I wanted to come off the Suboxone because of the side effects. While on Suboxone, using the bathroom was a nightmare. I was always constipated and had a lot of trouble urinating. Suboxone, as well as opioids such as heroin and OxyContin, also have a negative effect on a man's love life.

I stopped taking the Suboxone cold turkey. I didn't think it would be that difficult to come off Suboxone. I was wrong; dead wrong. After being on 24 mgs daily of Suboxone for over 6 months straight, the withdrawals were just as bad, if not worse, than OxyContin withdrawals. I tried to fight through it for 2 days, but the sickness became unbearable. Instead of taking more Suboxone to help with the withdrawals, I decided to call a friend to see if he could get me any OxyContin. I had not used in over 6 months, so I knew the high would be insane and eliminate all of my symptoms. Sure enough, I got my hands on some OxyContin in a matter of minutes. I broke up the entire 80mg pill into a fine powder and split it up into 4 lines. I snorted one of the lines and knew I was doomed as soon as I tasted the Oxy in the back of my throat. I was hooked.

I realized a few things that night. I was having trouble sleeping and not feeling the way I used to about selling weed and taking bets. I used to love it, but I started to question myself about it. It wasn't exciting anymore. Maybe some of it had to do with my being in love and knowing that if my girlfriend found out I was using or dealing drugs, she would leave me. I thought about giving it all up, but as soon as I snorted that one line of OxyContin, my worries about giving up the life and going straight edge were gone: long gone.

I realized that living a dirty lifestyle and trying to stay sober was not a possibility for me. I had a conscience, but it was completely suppressed when under the influence of drugs.

In less than a month, I was back at it again, and worse than ever before. My girlfriend watched helplessly as I continued to abuse drugs and throw my life away. My 23rd birthday came around in September of 2010. I lost $10,000 playing blackjack and my girlfriend broke up with me on the same night; this wasn't exactly the birthday present I had expected. A week later was the night I am confident I overdosed after an insane night of OxyContin, cocaine, Red Bull, vodka, and high stakes blackjack at the Tropicana Casino in Atlantic City. I wish I took a picture of what I looked like that morning. I was unrecognizable. Even worse, the first thing I did that morning after waking up in a pile of my own vomit was snort the rest of the OxyContin I had left. Not an overdose, not a near death experience, not anything would scare my disease straight.

A few weeks after I turned 23, I bought a bunch of Oxys with my friend, Dan. His parents were away, so we planned on snorting Oxys at his house all night. We broke up most of the pills we had into one big pile of powder. We were breaking off lines and snorting them all night. I was unaware that Dan was mixing in Xanax with the Oxys. I had not used Xanax in a long time, so I did not have the same tolerance for Xanax as I did for Oxy.

Suddenly, it was 2a.m., and I awakened abruptly when my head slammed on the steering wheel of my Acura RSX. I passed out at the wheel, drove off the road, and totaled my car after I plowed through a brick mailbox down the road from my parents' house. I somehow managed to make it home, but my car was destroyed.

I called Dan and told him what happened, and he came right over. My brother, Johnny, came outside and saw me standing next to my totaled car. I was so messed up that night that I looked worse than the wrecked car.

Johnny said, "Um, Steve, your front license plate is missing." I immediately jumped into Dan's jeep with Johnny, and we drove slowly down the road to the crash site. Sure enough, there was my license plate along with debris from my car next to the mailbox I destroyed. I threw the license plate and car parts into the trunk of Dan's car, and we sped back to my parents' house.

The next morning, I woke up to my dad screaming at me. He told me to get dressed, and we drove down to the house where I crashed my car. My dad walked me up to the front door and made me ring the door bell and confess to what I had done. I told the owner of the home that I drove off the road late at night and hit his mailbox, but I didn't mention anything about being under the influence. I paid him for the damages and that was the end of it, but it was the beginning of the darkest days of my life.

The following 13 months of my life is when I lost contact with most of my friends. My family didn't even know who I was anymore. A lot of people were scared of me, and with good reason. Had I met that dark person I was from the ages of 23 to 24 today, I would definitely be scared. I lost any love and compassion I had in my heart. I lost myself completely.

In the fall of 2010, the 80mg OxyContin pills that I fell in love with disappeared. Purdue Pharma, the pharmaceutical company that put this drug on the market, redesigned the pill into a gel form so it couldn't be crushed into a fine powder and injected or snorted. I was beyond angry when this happened. The next best thing was 30mg Oxycodone pills. On the street, they were called Roxys or blues. They came in multiple versions, but all had the same effect. Before the OC 80 pills were taken off the market, Roxys were very cheap. Once the OC 80's were gone, the street price of Roxys skyrocketed. I found myself a solid connection, Victor, who lived in Suffern. I became very close with him; Victor was a full blown heroin addict. He didn't snort heroin or OxyContin like I did; he used needles. He was the first person I ever saw shoot up heroin. Victor made me inject him a few times because he was having trouble finding a vein to hit. As I delved further into the drug underworld, I started to meet some immensely sketchy characters. Walking into a room and seeing someone stick a needle in their arm became normal to me. Somehow, I resisted the urge to turn to the needle. I was very close to trying it a few times, but never pulled the trigger. I am very grateful for this. It becomes significantly harder to kick a dope habit once you are a shooter. Major health issues can also come with injecting heroin or Oxy, issues I never had to worry about as a snorter.

In May of 2011, Victor was arrested on drug charges at a concert. He had multiple prior narcotics convictions and had already been to prison once before. He told me several times that he wasn't ever going back to prison. He was sentenced to 4-8 years in state prison. In October of 2011, Victor hanged himself and was found dead in his jail cell.

CHAPTER 30
Straight to the Source

There's a saying that when one door closes, another opens. In May of 2011, the doors of the Sullivan County Jail closed behind Victor, and they would never open again. But when the doors closed for Victor, the gates of hell opened for me.

Coincidentally, the same day Victor was arrested, I received a call from one of my friends telling me he found a Roxy connect that claimed he could get me as much as I wanted. I asked all the people I knew who were involved with drugs to let me know if they found a solid connection for Oxys. Most of the time I got calls about a reliable connection, it did not pan out, but this one was more than true. I had to go through my friend the first few times I dealt with this guy. My friend was not a drug dealer, and he could not take the stress of being a middle man with the number of pills we were moving. Eventually, I was introduced to the dealer directly.

The first time I met this guy, I knew there was something different about him. He was a professional criminal. I will not use his name or even say where he is from; that is how seriously dangerous he was. I got a very different vibe from this guy than any previous dealer. He was the first Oxy dealer I knew who did not use the pills at all. He was not selling to support his habit like me and every other dealer had done in the past. Rather, he was selling for straight profit, and he meant business.

I went to Atlantic City with him one weekend and he let out a few secrets in the hotel room while he was drunk. He talked about what he did for a living, who he was involved with, and how he was able to get his hands on so many Roxys. He claimed to have a line of dirty doctors who wrote out numerous prescriptions each month in exchange for cash. He said there were multiple mom and pop pharmacies that gave him unopened bottles of 500 Roxys straight from the manufacturer. I knew this was true because a few times a month, I would get those unopened bottles directly from the manufacturer. He even claimed to have a friend who was a narcotics officer who would give him whatever he picked up off dealers and addicts on the street.

I was buying between 5,000 and 6,000 30mg Oxycodone pills (Roxys, blues) off my dealer each month. I was paying on average $14 per pill, which means I was purchasing nearly $100,000 worth of Roxy a month. At least 900 of those were put aside for my own personal use. I used at least 30 pills a day. I also had a few people who got regular prescriptions of 120 pills each month and sold them to me.

One day, I was driving back from New York City down the Palisades Parkway after picking up 1,200 Roxys. All of a sudden, an unmarked police car pulled out behind me. The car followed me for miles until I crossed the border from New Jersey into New York, then the car made a U-turn and went back in the other direction. I let out a huge sigh of relief. This was getting to be old news for me.

When I got home that night, I started to really think about what I was doing and the risks I was taking. I did not like the man I had become. I could barely look at myself in the mirror. But every time I looked for a way out, it always came back to my opioid habit. I tried everything to kick it, and now I was worse than ever. I was buying Roxys in bulk for $14 a pill and selling them for $25. Most other dealers on the street were selling them for $30. That is $1 per milligram. If I stopped selling and had to buy them off small time dealers, I would have a minimum of a $900 a day habit. I knew I had to keep doing this; I could not see a way out.

In the summer of 2011, my parents sat me down and told me they could not live this way anymore. It wasn't the average screaming arguments that we had; we were all very calm. They told me I had until October 1st to get out and find my own place. I didn't argue with them, and started to look for my own apartment. I found a one bedroom condo with a one car garage to rent in Mahwah, New Jersey. It came with a price tag of $1,700 a month. I signed the lease in August of 2011 and was set to move in on October 1st. It worked out because the tenants who were currently living there were moving out September 30th.

My friend Ryan and his sister had an end of summer party that many of my high school friends were planning to attend. At this point in my life, I didn't like going to parties. I was rarely invited to any type of gathering anymore, but Ryan was a friend who I never lost. He told me recently that other people, even some of my close childhood friends, used to ask him why he was still friends with me. He told me that since I never did anything to harm him or any of my friends, he was not going to turn his back on me. I never stole from my friends or slandered them. In reality, I was hurting myself the most. Certainly, I was my own worst enemy. That being said, I do understand why my friends chose not to be around me. I was a sick person with an awful disease.

When I walked into Ryan's party, I felt awkward instantly. Most of my friends from high school had already graduated college and were starting out in the workforce. I hated having to answer the question, "So what are you doing; are you working?" My response would usually be something like, "I am just trying to stay out of trouble."

I saw a girl I used to hook up with from time to time. She was the kind of girl who loved to party, but only did it every once in a while. We used drugs together several times in the past. We started talking and catching up. I was upfront with her about what I was doing with my life. Towards the end of the night, she asked me if I could drive her home. I never drank alcohol towards the end of my addiction, so I was one of the few people at the party who wasn't drunk. I was high on Oxys 24/7, but there is no breathalyzer for that.

As soon as we got in the car, she asked if we could go back to my house to smoke. My parents were away that weekend and my brothers were not home. Other than Nana, I had the house to myself. We went upstairs into my room and I started rolling a blunt. She was very curious and began looking around my room. All of a sudden, she got this big smile on her face and asked, "Is that a money counting machine." I replied, "Yes." She was so excited by this and asked if she could play with it. I went into my closet and pulled out $10,000 in 20 dollar bills. I showed her how it worked and she began running the bills through the machine. This machine was top of the line and even had a counterfeit bill scanner. I handed her a fake $20 bill I had and told her to stick it somewhere in the middle and run it through. The machine could hold up to 250 bills at a time in the hopper. Sometimes 250 bills would fly through in a matter of seconds. As soon as it hit the counterfeit bill, the machine stopped and started beeping. She loved it.

Then I broke out some Roxys for myself, and she asked if she could have some. She told me she snorted blues a few times in college. Things got really crazy that night. She slept over and I drove her home that next morning.

CHAPTER 31
He Knows if You've Been Naughty or Nice

October 1, 2011 to December 24th, 2011 were the darkest days of my life. I moved into my own condo, and I was living by myself and using and selling an absurd amount of drugs. I was running a sports book which was bringing in tons of money each week. I went to a casino practically every weekend. I was involved with the type of people I had no business knowing.

Even at my worst, I was not an inherently violent person. But the people I was associating with were willing to do almost anything to protect their money and their freedom. I saw a lot of bad things happen over drugs and gambling money. I was scared of who I had become, and even more frightened of the company that I kept. I had a bad feeling that someone was going to try to rob me or even kill me. I slept with a bat in my hand every night. I held on to it the way a little boy holds onto his favorite teddy bear to feel safe. I also kept a knife on the table next to me. I was having nightmares all the time about either getting robbed by violent criminals or arrested by the police. If my nightmares ever came true, I would most certainly be sharing a jail cell with the likes of criminals seen on television shows. The lifestyle I was living was no longer fun. It was deadly serious.

I talked to my dealer about possibly getting a handgun for protection. There was no way I could get a handgun legally, I would have had to buy it on the streets. My dealer talked me out of it. He said getting caught with drugs and money is one thing. Getting caught with drugs, money, and guns is something very different. He told me I was being paranoid and that no one was coming to rob or kill me. I needed to focus on avoiding the police.

I already knew what the legal consequences would be if I were to get arrested with an illegal handgun in my possession. The few people I talked to about getting a handgun all had the same answer. "You are being paranoid. If you get caught with a gun, you're screwed." I really didn't want one anyway, but something inside of me kept giving me this feeling that I needed one. This would of course become a self-fulfilling prophecy.

On December 23, 2011, I went out to a bar with a few friends. I came home just after midnight on Christmas Eve. I pulled into Paddington Square, the condominium where I lived, and as I was about to turn onto my street, I saw a line of police cars. The cars were not parked directly in front of my house, so I was not sure if they were there for me. I saw my front door was wide open and the lights were on inside my condo. My heart sunk. This was it. I kept driving past my house and no one stopped me. I could have kept driving and tried to get out on another street, but I decided to turn around and drive back. A female Mahwah Police Officer signaled for me to stop and came up to my window. She asked if I was the resident at 1505 Cornwall Road. I told her I was. I was expecting her to say, "Get out of the car and put your hands behind your back, you're under arrest," but she didn't. The officer told me that 4 people tried to break into my apartment. A few more police officers came over and told me they broke my back window and a neighbor dialed 9-1-1 as soon as it happened. The Mahwah Police caught the two guys who tried to break into my apartment as well as the two people sitting in the getaway car down the road.

Of course, my next question was, "Who tried to break into my apartment?" Two other police officers came over and told me to pull my car into the driveway. They brought over the drivers' licenses of the quartet and asked me if I recognized any of them. I went through the first 3 licenses and looked at the names and photos. I did not recognize any of them. Then I looked at the last one, and I could not believe what I saw. A picture of one of my friends' dad, Richard Matera Sr., stared me right in the eyes. I played hockey with his son, and he had come to my apartment just a few weeks earlier. When he visited, he told me that his dad said hello. His father, Richard Matera Sr., was the fourth person in the group. I knew

Rich Sr. was involved in drugs. I had sold marijuana to him several times, but I never thought he would do something like this.

The two men who tried to break into my house were caught with a large hunting knife and rope. Their plan was to break into my apartment and steal my drugs and money. If they could not find money or drugs, they were going to wait for me to get home, beat me, tie me up, and torture me until I told them where my stash was. I learned that the two men who were on foot that night and planning on breaking into my apartment had long criminal histories. These guys were serious violent criminals willing to do anything to get my drugs and money.

The police were being very courteous to me and did not ask any questions about why I thought these people picked my apartment to burglarize. I was told that my house was a crime scene so I would not be able to sleep there. The officers said they were waiting for a detective to come down who was going to ask me a few questions, and then I could go. I was almost certain that the police were just stringing me along until the detective came down, but I hoped that they thought this was a random break-in and had no idea how my lifestyle fit into the equation.

The police went into my house to make sure there was no one hurt inside. I knew the only thing that was even suggestive of illegal activity was the money counting machine on my desk. It wasn't illegal to have a money counting machine, so I was not worried.

I thought that the police knew this was clearly not a random break-in and that there was likely illegal activity going on inside the residence, but they didn't have any evidence to arrest me. I thought maybe they were just being nice to me to convince me they were not going to start investigating me after this incident. I had a considerable amount of drugs and money inside. I usually hid my contraband in a vent in the laundry room, but I was only planning on staying at the bar for a short while, so I left everything in my coffee table drawer. Still, the only reason the police were legally allowed to enter my residence was due to the exigent circumstances of someone possibly being hurt or under distress inside. No person could be hiding in a coffee table drawer.

Once the detective showed up, the police were not so kind anymore.

The detective did not waste any time getting to the point. He told me he knew there were drugs and money in the house, and wanted me to sign a waiver allowing the police to search my residence without a warrant. I said absolutely not and asked for my attorney. I was brought down to the police station for questioning, but I was able to make a phone call and get word to my father that I was at the Mahwah Police station. He arrived not just as my father, but as my attorney as well. Since the police could not charge me with a crime until they got a warrant signed by a judge, they had to release me.

I went back to my parents' house in New York. I called my criminal defense attorney, David Goldstein, that morning. A few hours later he called and said the police got a warrant and found everything inside my residence. The Mahwah Police seized an electronic currency counter, three cut straws I used to snort my Oxys, a digital scale, Ziploc bags of rubber bands, a notebook, and my laptop. Oh yeah, they also seized 848, 30mg Oxycodone pills and $34,808 in cash.

I was charged with possession with intent to distribute Oxycodone and money laundering. I turned myself in 3 days later when I had all of my affairs in order. My bail was set at $100,000. I walked in with my attorney, was processed, posted bail, and was out the door in less than 30 minutes. A few days later, I went into a 7-day detox program called Sunrise. From there, I went to Mountainside, an inpatient program in Connecticut.

I was full of fear after the events that transpired on Christmas Eve. What would have happened if I were home that night? What if the neighbor did not hear the sound of breaking glass and never called 9-1-1? Would they have let me live or would they have killed me? Those thoughts raced through my head, and I was unable to turn them off.

To make matters worse, I was coming off a 900mg a day Roxy habit that lasted for 15 straight months. I couldn't eat or sleep, and I had no energy. Lastly, I was facing some very serious criminal charges. I was charged with possession with intent to distribute in the 2nd degree. If convicted, I faced a minimum of 5 years and a maximum of 10 years in prison. This was the perfect storm.

I got a call from my attorney while in treatment at Mountainside. He told me the prosecutor was offering to knock the charges down from a second to third degree charge, and that I would not have to do any jail or prison time. The bad news was that I had to plead guilty to an indictable offense and serve 2 years probation. I was curious as to why the prosecutor was offering no jail time so quickly. Goldstein told me and my dad that there were some serious issues with the police report. The arresting officer claimed he entered the apartment to see if anyone was in distress, and he then saw the drugs in a drawer on the way out of my apartment. I was definitely guilty of the crimes I was charged with that night, but was the evidence obtained illegally? I could have fought the charges and gone to a suppression hearing, but the risk was too high. If I lost, the plea deal would be off the table, and I could end up in prison for 10 years. I wasn't willing to take that chance.

I pleaded guilty to possession with intent to distribute Oxycodone on February 2, 2012. I became a convicted felon on that day. I drove over to the Bergen County Department of Probation after sentencing and met with a probation officer who transferred my case to be monitored by Rockland County, New York.

The staff at Mountainside urged me to admit myself into an extended care program. I wanted to move back to California, but my probation officer told me I was not allowed to leave the state. I was discharged from Mountainside in February of 2012, and moved back in with my parents. I met another resident in Mountainside who lived in Mahwah, New Jersey. We met up at Applebee's 3 days after I got home. We both ordered beers. Before I finished my third beer, we left Applebee's to go cop Roxys. That's how fast it happens for me.

I was never much of a drinker, but every time I get a few beers in me, I immediately start to crave opioids. This is why I do not drink anymore.

Within a few weeks, my tolerance went back to where it was before I got arrested. I did not want to get involved in dealing drugs again, but I spent over $20,000 in just over a month on my Roxy habit. My gambling business fell apart when I got arrested and was away in treatment. I had no money coming in, and a lot going out. With the money and drugs seized by the police, cost of attorney's fees, treatment, and fines, I lost over

$100,000. Then I spent $20,000 my first month out of treatment. I was running out of money fast, so I did the only logical thing someone with an addicted brain would do. I reconnected with my Roxy dealer and opened up shop again.

Now I was selling and using drugs on felony probation. There were no boundaries that could contain me. I needed to feed the beast, my disease of addiction was raging onward regardless of my predicament. The court took away my driving privileges in the state of New Jersey. I lived on the border of New York and New Jersey, so I had to be careful that I did not cross the border by accident.

My uncle Rich (Cook) called me one night to see if I wanted to come over for dinner and to watch the TV series, *Breaking Bad*. He lived in Ramsey, New Jersey with my aunt and cousins, so I told him I was not allowed to drive to his house. He responded rather quickly and said, "Let me get this straight. You will get high and sell drugs on felony probation but you won't drive a mile over the border to come hang out with your family?" Driving in New Jersey to go hang out at my cousin's house was a risk that did not serve my addiction, so I did not take it. I never broke the law unless the act supported my drug addiction. That is the way my brain worked.

Cook then said, "So maybe if you get the help you need to treat your addiction, then you will never need to break the law at all." I believed him when he told me I would have no issues with the police if I were able to get sober, but that seemed impossible for me.

My father said something similar to me months earlier after I was pulled over and searched by the police. I came home screaming, "The police are always following me and pulling me over. This is harassment!" My dad looked at me shaking his head and in a sarcastic tone and said to me, "I have some groundbreaking information for you. This is going to blow your mind, are you ready? Stop breaking the law, and maybe, just maybe, the police will stop bothering you." At the time, my addicted brain was infuriated with his comments, but that's because he was right.

In August of 2012, I convinced my probation officer to let me go to New Orleans for my brother Mike's bachelor party. I was already caught with dirty urine once by my probation officer, and she made me check myself into detox at Good Samaritan Hospital, the same hospital where I was born. A lot can change in over two decades. I knew when I was going to be meeting my probation officer a month in advance, so I would stop using 36 hours before to make sure I got the opioids out of my system.

I smuggled 150 Roxys on the plane with me on the ride to New Orleans. I also brought $8,000 cash to gamble at Harrah's Casino which was across the street from our hotel. I lost it all playing blackjack the first night. We went to the casino at 4a.m. and I was blackout drunk and high on Roxys. I barely remember losing the money. All I knew was that I woke up broke the next morning.

I was miserable the rest of the trip. We came home from Mike's bachelor party and I met up with my dealer to buy 1,000 Roxys. Just a few days later, my parents took my brother K to a hockey tournament. It was just me and Nana for the weekend. In the early afternoon on Friday, September 7th, 2012, I was sitting by my bedroom window smoking a cigarette. I was nodding out resting my elbow on the window sill with my hand on my face. All of a sudden, I heard the sound of loud car engines and squeaking wheels. I looked up and there was a line of cop cars flying up my driveway. It was a raid.

Multiple officers jumped out of the cars and ran into my house. I had over 600 Roxys in my closet. By the time I got to my closet, the cops were already in my bedroom. I was busted. They threw me on the ground and multiple officers jumped on my back. They threw the cuffs on me tight and brought me downstairs. They asked me where the drugs were, and I just put my head on the table. A few minutes later an officer came down and proudly declared to the rest of the officers, "We got him!"

I went through the all too familiar booking process, and was arraigned by a judge that evening. My bail was once again set at $100,000. No one from my family showed up that night to bail me out, so I had to spend the night in the county jail. The Rockland County Sheriffs came to Ramapo Police Headquarters to transport me to the Rockland County Jail. I had never been to jail before. An overnight at the station was the most jail time I had ever served.

The intake process at the jail was a surreal experience. This was the lowest point in my life, and I felt like I would have been better off dead. For the correction officers, it was business as usual. Fingerprints, mug shots, strip searches, taking of property, issuing orange jumpsuits, and never-ending questions in a damp and cold building that reeks of pain. The entire process took hours, going from one room to the next. After I saw the nurse, one of the corrections officers escorted me to my dorm. I was on the bottom bunk of a small bed with no pillow and a tiny little pad that served as a mattress. I did not get into bed until 3a.m. I was coming down from my last high, and exhausted from the terrible day. I fell asleep instantly.

The next morning, I woke up hoping what had happened the day before was just another one of my ominous dreams. To my disappointment, my nightmare was real. I looked around and there were several inmates in orange jumpsuits sizing me up. A few of them came over to me and asked me what I was in for. Before I could get settled, a corrections officer came over and said, "Stephen Hill, pack your shit, you made bail." I walked out of the jail and my mom and Cook were there waiting for me.

My mom told me she already spoke to Goldstein, and he said I had to enter into a treatment facility immediately or else I would be remanded to the Bergen County Jail on a probation hold for violating the terms of my probation. My mom drove me home to pack some clothes for treatment. As soon as I got home, I ran upstairs to see if the cops overlooked two small stashes I had hidden in my room. To my disappointment, I was cleaned out.

My addiction was screaming and cursing at me to figure out a way to get high. I started to freak out, so I sat down on the floor of my bedroom, leaned against my dresser, put my hands over my face, and started to cry. I was broken, and had no idea how to fix myself. I thought my life was beyond repair, completely shattered. I didn't think recovery was even a possibility for someone like me.

The next day, I got into a state-run treatment facility called Blaisdell in Orangeburg, New York. This was yet another 28-day program. Mike's wedding was just a few weeks away. If I left the treatment facility before the 28 days, I would be thrown in jail. After days of back and forth between my parents, attorney, probation officer, and case manager at Blaisdell, my probation officer agreed to let me leave for my brother's wedding provided I returned to a treatment facility by Monday morning. This was supposed to be a very happy time for my family, but my addiction was sucking the joy right out of it.

I left Blaisdell on September 27th so I could make it to the rehearsal dinner. I got wasted. The next morning, I woke up with an awful hangover. My brain knew exactly how to get rid of that hangover: Oxycodone or heroin. Unfortunately for me, the cops cleaned me out. All of the money I had left was spent on bail, and I had no drugs. This was the first time I was ever in this situation. The majority of full-blown drug addicts wake up broke with no drugs every morning. This was a first for me.

I was able to scrape up a few hundred dollars to try and buy some Roxys to get me through the day. I couldn't call my dealer because he only dealt with large scale shipments. I tried my hardest to find some Roxys, but came up short. I even debated taking a quick drive down to Paterson to score some heroin, but I knew my family would disown me if I got arrested down there after everything they did to get me to Mike's wedding. I called it quits. I said to myself I was going to drink alcohol and not do any drugs on the night of Mike and Camy's wedding.

After the ceremony, I started taking shots at the bar to get rid of the hangover I still had from the night before. I ended up having a great time at the wedding. I went back to the hotel and sat at the bar by myself. At 3:00a.m. on September 29th, 2012, I took my last drink. I haven't touched a drink or a drug since. September 30th, 2012 is my sobriety date.

CHAPTER 32
The Turning Point

I ended up going back to Mountainside on Monday morning after the wedding. I did not go into Mountainside thinking that I was ready to stay sober and turn my life around, I just had no other option. I lost everything and was now facing felony charges in two different states. I knew by the time this court case and round of treatment was done, I would be dead broke, and I was. I had nowhere left to turn.

I walked into the aftercare office at Mountainside and said, "Tell me what to do." The counselor in charge of aftercare used to be my counselor the first time I arrived at the facility. He knew me well and believed that I would certainly relapse without long term care. Until this point, I had been to 1 wilderness program, 6 inpatient programs, 2 outpatient programs, 3 detox centers, and saw multiple counselors, psychiatrists, and psychologists. Nothing worked, and I was worse than ever. It really seemed as if there was no hope for me and that there could only be two endings to my story. I would either be locked up in prison or 6 feet under.

The aftercare team at Mountainside recommended I go to a place in New Haven, Connecticut called Turning Point. Today, the program is called Turnbridge, but I always refer to the program as Turning Point. The program has changed since I was a resident there, so I will be speaking from my experience at the facility. This was one of the places recommended the last time I went to Mountainside. Again, I did not want to go to Turning Point, but I had no other options. I went there after my 28 day stay at Mountainside. One of my friends from Mountainside, Eric, came to Turning Point a few weeks after I arrived. We became very close friends throughout our stay at Mountainside, and it made me more comfortable knowing that I would not be alone.

I learned a little bit about what the Turning Point program was all about when I spoke to someone who worked at the Admissions Office. He told me it was a 3 phase step down program, meaning that residents would earn more freedom and trust from the staff as they progressed through the program. There is a residential and clinical side to the program as well as 12-step integration throughout the community.

I never went to extended care before arriving at Turning Point. Living in a "sober house" in California was the most I ever experienced after an inpatient program. I still had no clue what I wanted from life, and if I even wanted to stay sober my first day at the new treatment facility. I went through the admissions process and was dropped off at the Phase 1 House. All the residents were out at their Friday activity playing paintball, so there were only staff members at the house.

I went around to the back deck and met a few staff members and the program director, John Palmer. John introduced himself to me and was already familiar with my situation. He had a bit of news for me, bad news. He told me that the Bergen County Department of Probation only gave me a 30-day pass out of state and that they wanted me back in court on Monday morning. My parents were planning on keeping me at Turning Point for the full year as was recommended, but it looked like I was only going to stay for a few days since I used 28 out of my 30 days at Mountainside.

John told me that my father and my attorney were working on the situation and I had to stay put for the time being. John asked me about the specifics of the criminal charges I was facing, so I told him everything I was involved with and about the seriousness of my charges. He replied, "So you have felony cases in New York, you have felony cases in New Jersey, and you're in treatment in Connecticut. That sounds like some tristate unmanageability to me. Are you ready to get sober son?" As I got to know him better, I realized he dropped zingers like that all the time.

When the residents got back from paintball, I had to introduce myself to the community. I started to get to know the guys I was going to be living with. I was also assigned a case manager for Phase 1 and would meet my therapist on Monday morning when I went to the clinical building for the Intensive Outpatient Program (IOP). That would only happen if my attorney could convince the court to let me stay.

Monday morning came and my attorney was going in front of the judge to ask the court to allow me to remain at Turning Point. My entire legal situation was a nightmare. My felony probation was being monitored by Rockland County in New York for a conviction in Bergen County, New Jersey. I violated my probation in New Jersey by getting re-arrested in New York. I had two probation officers, one in each state, but only reported to one until I got re-arrested. It was all too confusing and stressful to think about, so I stopped worrying about the situation once I realized that everything was out of my control. My fate was in the hands of the judge.

David Goldstein convinced the judge to let me stay in treatment. Later on that day, I got the great news. I was so relieved. At that moment, I realized how strange it felt to be happy that I was allowed to stay in treatment. This was a change, and a first for me. I was not sure if that was due to the alternative to jail or because I wanted to give recovery a real shot. Either way, it was progress.

The next day, I was called into the Executive Vice President's office. Brett Tiberio introduced himself and talked with me for a little while. I learned that he was a graduate of the program and that going through Turning Point saved his life. Then, he got down to business. He handed me a waiver of extradition that was faxed over by my attorney that needed to be signed and sent back to the court immediately. This meant I was waiving my right to an extradition hearing if the state of New Jersey wanted me back in-state. If I did not appear in court or violated any of the terms of my probation, New Jersey could have me arrested and sent to the Bergen County Jail without a hearing. I signed the papers and let out another sigh of relief.

I started to get acclimated to the residents, staff, and day to day operations of the Turning Point program. I was in Phase 1 for 6 weeks. While a resident in Phase 1, your daily schedule is made for you. My days in Phase 1 would usually consist of the following: Wake-up, eat breakfast, do my chore, get in the van to be driven down to the IOP, take a drug test, participate in group therapy, go back to the house for lunch, go to the gym, have free time, attend a community meeting, eat dinner, and attend an outside AA or NA meeting. Then, go back to the house for a snack and check-in, and go to bed for lights out.

Some of those days would be broken up with other activities such as paintball, bowling, movies, sporting events, and trips to a museum. I also had a weekly individual session with my clinician and a weekly private session with my case manager. Sometimes my family would come up and visit on the weekends, and I would go out on pass for a few hours in the community.

Phase 1 started out very basic and expectations were at a minimum. I was assigned Continuing Care Plan (CCP) work by my case manager each week. Week 1 was about personal hygiene and the most basic tasks imaginable. I thought it was ridiculous at first, but then I saw other residents who had no clue how to make a bed, do laundry, sweep a floor, or other tasks I found commonplace. Some had to be told several times to shower and brush their teeth. I was a little taken aback by this. I assumed that everyone knew how to maintain personal hygiene and perform the most minimal of tasks. But when I was using, I was not taking care of myself. I would wait until I had no clean clothes left until I did laundry, I only brushed my teeth in the morning because I would fall into a drug induced sleep every night. I never made my bed, and I only cleaned my place when it was disgusting and unlivable.

Every Thursday night was the Turning Point AA meeting. All of the residents and many staff members would gather to celebrate clean time. I had 30 days sober at this point, but I did not want to get up for a coin. One of the Phase 3 residents kept pushing me to get a coin, and I eventually did. I got my 1 month coin, which honestly meant nothing to me at the time. I really didn't care. Whoever was handing out coins would start with anyone who had 24 hours clean. Next would be month by month until they hit the 1 year point. Then it was year by year. When a resident was celebrating 1 year at the Turning Point meeting, it was a huge deal. All the residents screamed and cheered for the people celebrating 1 year when it was their turn to speak and tell us how they did it. The resident's case manager would get up and say a few words on their behalf. I was certain I would never make it to 1 year of sobriety.

Eric, from Mountainside, was waitlisted on admission to Turning Point because they were at maximum capacity. After 3 weeks into my stay at Phase 1, he arrived. I was so happy to have him in the program with me. I introduced him to a few people I had met. Before long, I developed a close group of friends. Sometimes, I even forgot about the legal nightmare that was likely waiting for me once I completed the program. I knew even if I stayed sober and did all the right things for a year, I was still going to likely end up in prison, possibly in both New York and New Jersey. I tried my best not to let this get to me, but sometimes the anxiety of the unknown overwhelmed me.

One day, when my therapist Meaghan was running a group in IOP, she said she was going to put us all to sleep with hypnosis. I didn't believe she could actually do that. Sure enough, just about every resident was sound asleep within minutes, and I was one of them. I talked with her after about it and how my aunt had tried hypnosis to quit smoking. Meaghan said she could try it on me to help me quit smoking. I never had an open mind about anything like this, but somehow, she got it to work. Just before the end of my stay in Phase 1, I quit smoking cigarettes.

After my 6 weeks in Phase 1, I packed my bags and moved over to the Phase 2 house down the road. I was assigned a new Phase 2 case manager, Sam Cohen. He and I got along really well. While in Phase 2, I actually looked forward to my weekly sessions with him and Meaghan. I started to trust Meaghan by the time I was in Phase 2, and I started to open up to her. My number one fear and obstacle that we had to work through was my possible incarceration. The thought of prison was getting in the way of me buying into recovery. Love, helping other people, opening up, and doing the next right thing is what recovery is all about. But I did not want to fully commit to any of this, and I kept my guard up. I felt that everything that would help me in my recovery would hurt me if I had to survive in prison. I was much more focused on lifting weights and staying mentally prepared for the worst.

While in Phase 2, I started to volunteer at homeless shelters, churches, and other organizations. This was a requirement for the Phase 2 program. I also enrolled in 2 classes at Gateway Community College in downtown New Haven. Eric enrolled in the same DARC program with me. DARC stands for Drug & Alcohol Recovery Counselor. I wasn't sure if this was the career I wanted, but just getting back in school gave me some direction and purpose. This was the first time I ever attended college sober.

I took one DARC class and ENG 101. I had either failed or withdrew from ENG 101 many times before in 3 different colleges. I was starting to make positive changes in my life, but I was far from being out of the woods. Just before I started class in January of 2013, I started to feel terrible back pain. The pain was shooting up and down my legs. I thought maybe I injured it in the gym, but the pain was not going away. I was still having trouble sleeping as my body was still trying to adjust. When I was using, I never actually went to sleep; I would just nod off and pass out randomly throughout the day and night.

It was the middle of the winter, and I had to carry around a backpack with 3 shirts because I was sweating profusely throughout the day. I tried multiple types of anti-perspirant deodorants. Nothing was working. I started to have tooth pain as well. Most of these ailments and issues were probably with me for quite some time, but I never felt them because I was high on Oxycodone 24/7. The mood swings, constant sweating and trouble sleeping were a direct result of my body detoxing. I found myself getting irritated easily and having drug dreams more often. I brought this up in one of my sessions with Meaghan, and she told me I was going through PAWS, Post-Acute Withdrawal Syndrome. In my opinion, PAWS is one of the leading causes for relapse. I was starting to feel better sober, but then, all of a sudden, I started to feel worse. The symptoms of PAWS for an opioid abuser can last up to 2 years. The symptoms decrease as time goes on and there are ways to shorten it such as exercising and eating healthy.

My criminal cases were being pushed back while I was in treatment, so I didn't have to appear in court. I was allowed to go on my first overnight for Christmas towards the end of my stay in Phase 2. This would be the first time I was back in my home since October. I was both nervous and excited to go back home to see my family. Christmas Eve is a big event for my Italian family, and there is always lots of drinking. My case manager asked my parents to speak with the rest of the family about having a dry Christmas. My parents talked to me about it separately, and I told them I would appreciate it if our family tried not to get wasted, but that telling everyone they can't drink because I am coming home on an overnight from rehab would make me feel even more uncomfortable.

I didn't want to be the burden who was ruining everyone's fun. I didn't want people to have to make adjustments for me, but everyone is different. Some people cannot be around alcohol at all in early recovery. Alcohol wasn't my thing, so it doesn't really bother me when people drink around me. I rarely have a craving to drink. If anything, being the only sober person around drunk people is just annoying. It really does put things in perspective, and I see how stupid even adults act when they are drunk. Watching a large group of drunk parents sing *Sweet Caroline* at a Fourth of July party was one of the most embarrassing experiences of my life.

My first sober Christmas Eve went well. I had gotten some color back in my face and had been lifting weights for 2 months, and it was starting to show. My family was complimenting me on my appearance. I was not used to that, nor was I used to receiving any kind of compliments at all for quite a while. When people spoke about me previously, it was almost certainly negative. On Christmas morning, my brother Johnny was still sleeping when everyone else was opening their presents. I was usually the one who came down last. I screamed up to Johnny, "Come on down; you have to show up for life." The look on my mom's face was priceless. She couldn't believe that I was telling someone else to show up for life. I hadn't shown up for life in a very long time. Things were starting to change.

When I got back to the Phase 2 house, I was breathalyzed and given a drug test upon arrival. My bags were taken by staff and searched thoroughly. I stayed in Phase 2 for 8 weeks, and then on February 1, 2013, I was moved to the final Phase of the program, Phase 3. I entered Phase 3 with just over 4 months of sobriety, the longest clean time I had since I picked up that first drug my freshman year of high school when I was only

14 years old.

I met my Phase 3 case manager, David Martinez (D-Mar), and went over the rules, regulations, and expectations. I already met the Phase 3 program director, Dave Murphy (Murph), a few weeks earlier when he drove me back to the Phase 2 house after the weekly Thursday night AA meeting.

The first thing I did was make my daily schedule with D-Mar. In Phase 3, residents had more freedom and flexibility in making their own schedule, but we still had to follow it as best as we could. If I wanted to deviate from my schedule, I would have to call D-Mar and get permission. Built into my schedule was volunteering 2 days a week, class 2 days a week at the community college, weekly meetings with my case manager, and weekly therapy sessions. I also had to participate in a Phase 3 group once a week at the clinical building, attend the Turning Point AA meetings on Thursday nights, take a minimum of 3 drug tests per week, attend six 12-step meetings a week, and 1 house meeting. Curfew was 10p.m. on weekdays, and 12a.m. on the weekends. If I wanted to go on a pass, I had to fill out a form and have it approved by my case manager.

I had a rough start in Phase 3. I missed my first house meeting because my ride to the gym was at the same time of the meeting. All Phase 3 residents had to figure out their own transportation. I either took the bus, got a ride from a staff member or found a Phase 3 resident who earned the right to have a car. I sometimes got rides from people in the recovery community who were not associated with Turning Point. I knew I would get in trouble if I missed the house meeting, but I did not care. When D-Mar called me to see where I was, I told him I was at the gym and would get there when I could, and then I hung up on him. He called back a few times, but I sent his calls straight to voicemail. I did not return to the house until later that night after I attended my AA meeting. I got a call early in the morning from D-Mar telling me to come downstairs to Murph's office. They were both sitting there waiting for me. As soon as I walked in the office, Murph asked, "Why aren't you at your volunteer commitment? It says on your schedule you are supposed to be there now." I told D-Mar and Murph that once school started, I stopped going to my volunteer commitments. I told them I felt this was beneath me, and that I just needed to focus on school.

Murph got up and walked out of the room. A few seconds later he opened the door again and said to D-Mar, "Maybe we should write a letter to the court letting them know that Stephen is not complying with the expectations of the program." He then declared that there would be no passes home and then said to D-Mar, "Write him up a behavior contract." Murph shut the door again, and I started screaming at D-Mar. I could not afford to have any negative progress reports with the criminal charges I was facing. Even if I did everything perfectly, the odds were still not in my favor. He calmed me down and explained that they were just trying to help me. He explained how lying and not showing up for commitments are signs of old behaviors that are not consistent with being a clean and sober man. I kept arguing with him about how I thought the house meetings were a waste of time, and we just talked about nonsense and how I would much rather go to the gym. He kept trying to calm me down because I was so heated about the court comment Murph made. D-Mar told me if I just followed the simple rules that we could avoid ever having these conversations again. He told me to go talk to some of the guys that had been in Phase 3 for a few months and were doing the right thing. He said I should ask them what their days were like now.

That night, two Turning Point graduates gave me a ride to my AA meeting. I vented everything that was going on with me and they pretty much had the same response. If I did the right thing, I would make it much easier on myself. I had to stop trying to rationalize and make sense of every aspect of the program and just go with it. Obviously, my way wasn't working. My way got me in the doors of Turning Point with a deadly drug addiction, felony cases pending, no college credits, no career, and no money. I used the last of my money to pay for some of the costs of Turning Point. By the time I was in Phase 3, I was dead broke and being fully supported by my parents.

My second week in Phase 3 was met with a huge snowstorm. I was living at the main Phase 3 residence on 1 Grand Avenue. We were snowed in for more than a day. Everyone was smoking cigarettes and vaping in the house. During my time stuck in the house, I went a little crazy and needed something to take the edge off. I started smoking cigarettes again.

I tried vaping a few times, but never got into it. Vaping and juuling are a huge problem in the recovery community. So many people started out vaping as a way of quitting cigarettes. This strategy has the complete opposite effect. The amount of nicotine intake from vaping is usually significantly more than smoking cigarettes.

Eric came into Phase 3 shortly after I arrived. Within just a few weeks of his being in Phase 3, he was given car privileges and was made house manager. It usually took months before someone was even considered for a house manager position, but the Phase 3 community was in a downward spiral at the time and they believed Eric could help turn that around. When I was in Turning Point, there were up to 6 Phase 3 houses. Each house had a Phase 3 resident house manager who was paid to watch over the facility. Being a house manager meant you were one of the most trusted residents. The job gives a resident purpose and structure and could lead to permanent employment upon successful completion of the program.

I was psyched when Eric got a car. The first time he came to pick me up I said to him, "This is amazing; we have a car now." Eric and I were with each other every day when we were residents. Now that we had a car, we started to date girls. In Turning Point, dating girls is not allowed. Not only Turning Point, but many professionals and people in recovery feel that you should not form any new relationships during your first year of sobriety. Eric and I followed this suggestion as best as we could. We may or may not have dated 2 girls we met at the community college while we were in Phase 3. Who remembers?

I received a new volunteer commitment helping out at the Turning Point clinical building downtown. I just. cleaned and helped the office manager with various tasks, but it gave me some responsibility. Each day of the week, I either had volunteer work or school, sometimes both. At one of my weekly sessions with D-Mar, he told me I was making great progress and brought up the idea of making me a house manager. The current house managers had weekly meetings with Murph and the Phase 3 facilities manager, Rob. D-Mar usually sat in on the meetings too. He told me that there was talk of making me the 1 Grand house manager once the current manager graduated from the program. Since I had a rocky start in Phase 3, some people were uncertain as to whether or not I would be a good fit for the job.

In the spring of 2013, I went with a few friends to an early morning AA meeting in West Haven. When the meeting ended, a bunch of the guys went to The Owl Shop in downtown New Haven to smoke cigars. It was there that I met an older man who would change my life forever. He was not affiliated with Turning Point in any way, but he was a very important member of the New Haven recovery community. I listened to him talk about life and mistakes he made, and I could relate to everything he said. I introduced myself to him and started telling him about how I ended up at Turning Point. He was a great listener. I got his phone number and began calling him regularly. He became my recovery mentor and sponsor, and still is to this day. He taught me what it means to be a sober man. For purposes of the second letter in AA, he will remain "anonymous."

In April of 2013, Turning Point began to put together its softball team for the Greater New Haven Sober Softball League. Eric was made captain and picked our squad. There were 8 teams in the league. Each team had to have 3 girls in the line-up. Eric and I got permission to go to a local women's sober house to recruit players. All the guys were really excited to play in this league. Most of my friends at Turning Point were athletes, and this gave us a little reminder of what life was like before we picked up drugs and alcohol, and we remembered how exciting and fun healthy competition could be.

At our first game, we mercy ruled the other team. We had a blast. I remember the feeling I had before, during, and after that first game. It had been years since I played any sport. This league was centered upon sobriety, and almost everyone in the league was in recovery. That night all of us went out to celebrate. I was happy and truly sober. All my legal troubles and other issues were put on hiatus that evening.

CHAPTER 33
A New Phase

In May of 2013, I found out I was going to be hired as the house manager for the main Phase 3 residence beginning June 1st. This was perfect timing for me as I finished my 2 classes at Gateway Community College. A house manager needed to have a car, so I leased a 2013 Nissan Altima before I was hired. I sold my Audi A4 a few months earlier and used all of the money to help pay for Turning Point. As the 1 Grand House manager, my responsibilities included the following: weekly shopping trips to BJ's to buy cleaning supplies for all of the Phase 3 houses, weekly trips to Walmart for Phase 3 residents to go food shopping, making sure all residents were in by curfew and breathalyzed upon arrival, and supervising the residents to make sure they were doing their chores. I also had to drug test all of the residents on either Saturday or Sunday.

I really enjoyed being the house manager. Since I was the one doing all the drug testing on the weekends, my boss, the facilities manager, drug tested me. Things were going really well for me. My back pain had gone away, and my sweating issues subsided. I was sleeping well at night without the assistance of medication. In fact, I believe Eric and I were the only 2 residents in Phase 3 who were not on any medication. Many people who suffer from addiction also suffer from a simultaneous mental health disorder. This is referred to as a dual diagnosis. It is not uncommon for an addict to begin taking drugs and self-medicating. If someone who has an undiagnosed anxiety disorder takes a Xanax for the first time, you might actually see an improvement in his or her behavior. People suffering no longer feel the anxiety while on Xanax, so they keep taking more. Then, they build up a tolerance to the drug and need to increase the dosage to achieve the same effect. This is where abuse can rear its ugly head. If not closely monitored by a doctor, the use of controlled substances can get out of control rather quickly. Even if patients are monitored by a doctor, these individuals can start scoring pills on the street if they are cut off by their doctors or run out of pills before their refill.

I am grateful that I did not have to take any medication while in recovery. I used non-narcotic sleeping pills while I was in detox and at Mountainside, but I decided not to take any medication while I was at Turning Point.

After I was hired as a house manager, I went to see Meaghan for my weekly therapy session. I walked in and told her the great news. She already knew and was very excited and proud of me. She also heard that I made the Dean's List at Gateway Community College. We sat down and she started listing all of my accomplishments and the great things she was hearing about me. Then she stopped and said, "Stephen, you have no idea how to accept a compliment, do you?" She couldn't have been more right. It had been so long since I did anything worthwhile, anything laudable. I was used to being talked about in a negative way, being put down, and being the guy no one wanted around. I actually became somewhat comfortable in this negative role. I knew all too well how to be the junkie or the felon, not the student or sober man. Being complimented for positive behavior was new to me, and I didn't know how to handle it. I have gotten more accustomed to positive comments, but I still struggle with it. I've been told that I make a weird grimace when someone compliments me. Some even say that it looks like I don't believe the nice things that people are saying.

I made some real progress in my first 8 months of recovery, but the light at the end of the tunnel was still dimmed by the fear of the unknown. Too many questions remained unanswered. Was I going to end up in prison? After putting my court cases off for almost a full year, Goldstein started to talk with the probation officers and prosecutors. We had 2 cases in 2 different states to work through. He told me to get a personalized letter from the program director talking about my accomplishments in the program. Many treatment facilities have a form letter they use for court appearances and just change the name on it. The letter I got was not the standard letter. John Palmer wrote an amazing and heartfelt letter to bring to the judges. Goldstein also asked me to talk with my boss about permanent employment at Turning Point after I completed the program. This could go a long way in keeping me out of prison and possibly allow me to stay in the Greater New Haven area. I developed a strong sober network and strong group of supportive friends in recovery in Connecticut, but there was a possibility I would have to live in the state of New York if my sentence was probation.

The first case we dealt with was the violation of probation on a felony conviction in New Jersey because I was re-arrested on felony charges in New York. My original sentence was 2 years probation, but now that could turn into a lengthy prison sentence. It was only about a year and a half when we went in front of the judge and I violated my probation; however, the letter written by John Palmer carried a lot of weight. John says that I give him too much credit for the letter he wrote, and that everything he stated was earned with hard work, doing the next right thing, and dedication to sobriety. Although this may have been accurate, he did not have to guarantee me full-time employment. Murph gave me a glowing recommendation when John asked him how I was doing as the house manager in Phase 3. I was truly blessed that so many people were helping me navigate through my legal issues.

Somehow, Goldstein convinced the judge, with the agreement of the probation officer, to dismiss my probation early. Maybe the Bergen County court figured that since my probation was already being monitored by Rockland County, New York, and I had pending charges there as well, they could just let New York deal with me. I'm not really sure what happened that day, but someone was looking out for me. My legal troubles in New Jersey were over in the summer of 2013. 1 case down, 1 to go.

Since I had never been convicted of a felony in New York, I thought I had a good chance of ending up in felony drug court or possibly Shock Incarceration. Felony drug court is an 18-month intensive program monitored by the court. It's much stricter than probation. Upon successful completion, my felony would be reduced to a misdemeanor. I would have to live in Rockland County if I were admitted into drug court. Shock Incarceration is a boot camp prison focused on treatment, education, and physical fitness. Neither option was appealing to me, but one of these seemed like the only outcome I could expect.

Goldstein called my father and told him that he was going to try to convince the prosecutors to sentence me to 2 years probation and transfer the probation to be monitored in Connecticut so I could live and work there. Going back home to New York with just a year sober and no job would be a dangerous decision. All of my drug friends and contacts lived in that area. Everyone I knew in Connecticut was sober. I was part of something bigger than myself at Turning Point and in the recovery community of New Haven. I knew this was my best shot at maintaining long term sobriety. My parents, the treatment team, my friends, and my lawyer were all on board with having me stay in Connecticut. Unfortunately, it was not going to be an easy task to convince the court to go along with my plan.

In August of 2013, I was given a discharge date from Turning Point; it would be September 30th, 2013. This was my 1 year sober date. Eric was given the same discharge date and was also offered a job working at the Turning Point clinical building. I was planning on moving into an apartment with him, but I was not sure if I was going to be able to because of my tenuous legal situation. I was eagerly awaiting the call from Goldstein. Finally, he called my father with the news. He was able to convince the prosecutor to let me stay in Connecticut. I would plead guilty to misdemeanor possession and be sentenced to 3 years probation. The judge still had to accept the plea offer, but things were looking good for me for a change.

I went to my first court date almost a year after I had been arrested. Goldstein went over to the prosecutor's table and chatted with them for a while. Goldstein is a tall man with decades of experience in criminal law. The 2 prosecutors looked fresh out of law school. I watched them closely as they listened to everything he had to say. Oddly, it almost looked as if he were their boss. Minutes later, the judge came out and I was the first one called. Goldstein spoke to the judge and told him about the plea agreement. The prosecutor signed off on it. Everything came down to the judge. He looked up at me and stated, "I am going to accept the plea agreement." I wanted to start jumping for joy, but I kept it under control until I got out of the courtroom. The judge instructed me to contact the Rockland County Probation Department and they would submit the transfer to Connecticut. I was given one last court date for sentencing.

I met with a probation officer and she took down all of my information and submitted it to the New Haven Adult Probation Office. Just when I thought I was out of the woods, Goldstein called and told me my probation transfer request to Connecticut was denied. For some reason, they would not accept a misdemeanor probation transfer. I thought I was going to have to move home to New York and give up my job working at Turning Point. Luckily, Goldstein had one last trick up his sleeve. He reasoned with the prosecutors and judge and explained that bringing me back to Rockland County could be detrimental to my recovery. It really did not make sense to deny me the chance to stay in Connecticut, and the court agreed. But the only way for me to live in Connecticut would be if the court agreed to not give me probation. Somehow, they agreed. It was over. In more ways than one, I was a free man.

I called my friends at Turning Point and told them the great news. The next day, I was called into John Palmer's office. He sat me down and said, "So you're not going to prison in New York, you're not going to prison in New Jersey, and you're not even getting probation. Also, we have decided to give you a full-time job here starting out in a management position. You will be given a salary and benefits. How does that sound?" Tears started streaming down my face as I sat in his office. We cracked a few jokes and I gave him a big hug. Before I walked out of his office, John said to me, "You may have one more high left in you, but I seriously doubt you have one more recovery. Take this miracle gift you have been given, and go do something extraordinary." I was given a second chance. My father would say it was more like my 90th chance, but this was the first time I was in a position to make a real life for myself. I was given a chance to live a life beyond my wildest dreams. I walked out of John's office that day with a brand new start.

CHAPTER 34
The Past Becomes the Future

I started working as the Phase 2 Support Staff Manager a week before I was discharged as a resident from Turning Point. I was in charge of about 15 support staff. I worked close to 50 hours a week and performed a variety of tasks. I loved working there, and decided to put school on hold while I was managing Phase 2.

Eric and I got our own apartment and moved in a few days before we celebrated our 1 year sobriety milestone. Eric's sobriety date is one day after mine. September 30th, 2013 fell on a Monday, so I got my coin a few days later at the Thursday night Turning Point AA meeting. I celebrated my year of sobriety with Eric and 2 other friends with all of our families in attendance. Today, 3 out of the 4 of us who received our 1 year coin that night are still sober.

I sat patiently as I waited for the person giving out the coins awarded to the month by month recipients. Soon after, he called out "1 year," and the place went wild as the 4 of us stood up to receive our coins. Even more special to me was that my sponsor was the speaker at the meeting after the coins were given out. I knew I had to go up and give a short speech, so I asked my sponsor what I should say. He told me to, "Just speak from the heart, kid." I did just that.

When the meeting ended, we went out with our families and celebrated. Later that evening, Eric and I went back to our apartment and sat outside talking. It was the first time I felt completely free in recent memory. I was officially discharged from Turning Point and working as a full-time staff member. I did not have any legal troubles for the first time in years. There were no pending cases, not even probation. What really made me feel free was knowing that with no one monitoring me, I still did not have the urge to pick up a drink or drug. I was relieved of the mental obsession that had taken over my life. I was no longer in the grips of my mistress, OxyContin. I ended my tumultuous relationship with her for good. That night, I realized I had crossed the threshold of wanting to be sober more than wanting to be high. I went into treatment because I had no other option. I went in mostly because of the criminal justice system. I came out a sober man who wants sobriety for myself, not others.

I went back to Suffern almost every Friday during the winter of K's senior year of high school to cheer him on at his Suffern Hockey games. He is such a talented player and it was such an amazing experience to be able to show up to his games to support him.

In the beginning of the summer of 2014, I was moved to a position as the Phase 3 manager. In the capacity of my duty as the Phase 3 manager, I was searching a resident's vehicle for drugs with another staff member. We were specifically searching for heroin. The car had already been searched once by a different staff member, but he came up empty. Based on the information I had, I was almost certain there was heroin in that car. When I went out to search the vehicle with another staff member who was my age and also in recovery, we asked each other, "What are some of the classic stash spots for drugs in a vehicle?" I ripped up the cup holder and there it was. There were about 20 bags of heroin scattered under the "secret compartment" under the holder.

This was the first time I had seen drugs since I had been in recovery. The feeling that came over me was immensely powerful and unnerving. I felt a euphoric sensation run throughout my entire body---it was instant. If someone could have taken an image of my brain at that moment it would have lit up like a Christmas tree. My first thought was to put a few in my pocket and save them just in case I "needed" them one day. That was an uncontrollable thought that came into my brain; old habits die hard. A third staff member came out, and we all had the same look on our faces. We were all recovering opioid addicts, and we all had the same feeling. I was relieved to not be alone in this. One of the staff members lightened the mood by saying, "Well, we don't want to speculate, so the first thing we should do is all snort just a little bit to make sure it's really heroin." The three of us started laughing hysterically.

I suggested that we go inside and "call the boss." As I put the 20 bags in my pocket and headed inside the facility, a New Haven patrol car drove by. My heart sunk. I thought, "Just my luck, I am going to get arrested for doing my job and finding heroin in a resident's car."

I was relieved to see the New Haven Police vehicle continue driving. I ran inside and called my boss, but he did not answer. I kept going up the chain until someone responded. I got in touch with one of the top guys at Turning Point. I told him what we found. He was smart enough to ask me if the other staff members and I were emotionally and physically okay. We threw the bags in the toilet and flushed them. I videotaped it on my phone to prove that they went down. Of course, one bag kept popping back up after the flush. It was almost as if the heroin were taunting us. We flushed it a second time to get the last bag down. Sure enough, it popped up again. Finally, on the third flush, the heroin was gone.

The three of us were unsettled by this for a few days. We talked about what it felt like to have so much heroin right there in front of our eyes. Two of us were graduates of Turning Point, and the other staff member was a house manager about to graduate the program. If something like that were to happen to me in my first few months of sobriety outside of a program setting, there is a high probability I would relapse. The other two agreed. We learned how to deal with situations like this, and we followed our training. Even so, there is no guarantee that all of us would not have decided to split the bags up and get high together. That is how powerful the disease can be. Addiction has the ability to take 3 recovering addicts and hurl them into the abyss at will. Not this time.

When this incident occurred, the house manager, Bill, was on leave from law school. He completed his first 2 years while abusing heroin and Oxycodone. How he was able to pull this off, even he doesn't know. I was Bill's boss as the Phase 3 manager, and we actually became close when I was the Phase 2 manager and he was a resident. We are from the same area and know some of the same people.

One day, we started talking about our career plans. Bill was interested in becoming a trial attorney. This always interested me, but I assumed with my history, there was no way I could make it past the character and fitness test. When he asked me what I wanted to do, I really was not sure. I was so relieved to not be in prison and have a job at Turning Point, I never thought that far into the future. I was living in a protective bubble for almost 2 years, and I thought it was time for a change.

I was 26 years old and had completed only 3 college classes. If I were ever going to attempt a return to school, this was the time. I talked about it with my parents, my sponsor, and my therapist, Meaghan. They were all supportive of my decision to go back to school full-time. I talked with a few people about how hard it would be to get past the character and fitness test since my goal was to complete my undergraduate degree and then attend law school.

Since I am a non-violent drug offender and all of my criminal charges were drug related, I would not be automatically disqualified from being admitted to the bar. I went back to New York and had a long talk with my parents. The idea of going to school part-time and working part-time was brought up, but I decided to leave work and go to school full-time. The only way this would work financially is if I moved back home with my parents. There was some concern about my moving back to my hometown and into the same house where my drug addiction began. I thought about it for a long time, and it was not an easy decision for me. I realized that I was not the same person who left home to go into treatment. I was a completely different person with solid recovery. In August of 2014, I gave my 2 weeks' notice at work.

I went home to New York and met with Wendy Gordon, a family-friend who is an advisor at Rockland Community College (RCC). Wendy tried to help me numerous times when I attempted to go to RCC during my drug addiction. There was nothing that she could do to help me academically given my condition at that time. I was now a sober man, and she helped me put together a plan to get through college and into law school as quickly as I could. I wanted to finish college in 3 years, so we put together a plan to make that happen. I went back to New Haven and finished my last week of work. Bill was being discharged and going back to finish his final year of law school the same week I was leaving to go back to New York. I said my goodbyes to my friends and co-workers, packed my stuff, and headed back to my parents in Suffern, New York.

CHAPTER 35
Progress, Not Perfection

Throughout my first year at RCC, I was asked to speak about addiction and sobriety to classes at a middle school and high school. I had done it a few times before when I was working in New Haven. John Palmer sent a few of us to a high school to speak to the students. I also went to speak to high school health classes with a sober man from the New Haven recovery community. I received a lot of positive feedback every time I presented at schools. In November of 2015, I was asked to speak at a town hall meeting with the focus on the prescription drug and heroin epidemic. I had spoken in front of large groups before at AA meetings and a few schools in Connecticut, but this was the first time it would be in front members of a community. I shared my story about my struggle with addiction and journey to recovery in front of over 500 people. Parents, students, teachers, police, medical professionals, and many others were in attendance that night.

A few months later, I spoke at another town hall meeting on the same subject. Then I was asked by the administration at Albertus Magnus High School and Clarkstown South High School to speak to the students at their schools on a Rockland County-wide substance abuse awareness day. The Clarkstown Teachers Association then had me speak at their own town hall meeting. I spoke at homeless shelters and support groups as well.

When I was a resident in Phase 1 at Turning Point, the staff took us to a high school in Connecticut to see Chris Herren speak. This man's story was extremely powerful, but his willingness to share it so openly was what really inspired me. Chris was a professional basketball player who destroyed his career and almost his life to drug addiction. He is famous, so it's harder for me to try to relate to what he experienced. However, seeing him front and center speaking to students inspired me to do the same.

After receiving my associates degree from RCC, I transferred to John Jay College of Criminal Justice. I was taking more than a full course load each semester as well as winter and summer classes in order to graduate in the Spring of 2017. I started to study for the Law School Admission Test (LSAT) in the summer of 2016. It was during this same time that I also started my own company, Speak Sobriety.

Through my experience of speaking at different venues the past few years, I put together a substance abuse prevention and awareness presentation for students, faculty, parents, and any members of a community. My presentation is not only about facts and statistics, it is also about my real life story. Through my own personal experience with substance abuse, working in the field of addiction, keeping up to date on current events, and speaking personally with students, faculty, and parents, I have been able to share my story in an educational and motivational presentation.

Since I have experienced just about everything related to substance abuse, I find a way to speak about these issues as they relate to my story. For the topics that I have not experienced personally, I talk about one of my friends or family members who has experienced a particular situation or issue.

I started marketing myself to schools in Rockland, Westchester, Suffolk, and Nassau County New York, as well as Bergen County, New Jersey. I sent out emails and pamphlets to schools and somehow managed to design my own website. I have no idea how I did it. If someone asked me to design my website twice, I would fail miserably the second time. I only had a few references, so I was trying to make something of myself on my own. Many people thought that I would be lucky to get even one school to book me to speak.

I was able to get into a few schools just on my word. One school in particular, Islip Middle School in Suffolk County on Long Island, really made a difference for me. The school social worker, Shari Pennington, went out on a limb and had me come in and speak to the 7th and 8th grade students at her school without ever hearing me speak or talking to any references. Just about every school that I was in contact with would not even consider having me as a speaker unless they came to preview my presentation at another school first.

Shari and I talked on the phone a few times, and she asked me a lot of questions before she committed to having me speak at the school. She believed in me as a sober man and role model for the students at Islip Middle School. I was not used to people giving me a chance, and I am eternally grateful to Shari for taking a chance on me.

More schools started bringing me in as a speaker during the 2016-2017 school year. Elwood-John Glenn High School, Nanuet High School, Midland Park Jr/Sr High School, and Washingtonville Middle School are just a few schools that truly believed in my program. When the faculty at the school supports me, and believes in my program, it really shows in the way the students receive my presentation.

I ended up speaking at over 20 middle schools, high schools, colleges, and community forums my first year. I made a lot of contacts and got my name out there for the years to come. Most of all, I was doing something that I loved to do and helping people at the same time. I had found my passion.

I was on pace to graduate with a Bachelor's of Science in Criminal Justice from John Jay College in the summer of 2017. I was scheduled to take the LSAT in February of 2017. I started submitting applications to law schools a few months earlier so they could be reviewed as soon as my score was released.

My brothers Mike and Johnny both did well on the LSAT. I am smart enough to know that I am not as intelligent as Mike or Johnny academically. Along with my dad, they read more than any other people I know, and they retain just about everything they read.

I did everything I could to prepare for the LSAT. The morning of the exam, I arrived at Bergen Community College where I would be taking the test. As I was sitting in the lobby on the morning of the test, I had what many people in recovery refer to as a "spiritual experience." I will never forget sitting there and thinking to myself, "How the fuck did I get here?" Usually, when I had that thought, I had gotten myself into a terrible situation. Not this time. The fact that I was about to take a test for admission to law school was truly a miracle. I started thinking about where I was in my life just over 4 years earlier. Even if I did not answer one question right on that day, the fact that I took the exam was a huge accomplishment for me.

I ended up getting an above average score on my LSAT. It was not as good as either of my brothers', but I was more than satisfied. I had a 4.0 GPA when I applied to law school and was confident I could keep that GPA all throughout college. More than any grade on my application, I had a compelling story to tell in my essay. It's safe to say that I have had more life experience than the average person who applies to law school, or any school for that matter.

Just a few weeks after I got my LSAT results, I received a letter of admission from Pace Law School with a considerable scholarship. Just knowing that I was going to law school was a huge relief for me. My number one choice was Brooklyn Law School. Johnny is currently a student there, and he loves it.

On April 11, 2017, I received my letter of admission for the entering class at Brooklyn Law School's 4 Year JD Program. I couldn't believe I was accepted. My family and I went out and celebrated. Everything seemed to be falling into place.

EPILOGUE
The Solution

I have a life today that I never thought was possible. I was beyond hopeless when I was in the clutches of active addiction. I have a great relationship with my supportive and loving family. I have true friends, the ability to help others, a career path, and live a happy and healthy lifestyle. But the most important thing that I have in my life today is my sobriety. More than anything else, my sobriety has to come first. If I lose my sobriety, I will lose everything good in my life.

There was a point in my addiction when I considered myself a lost cause. Countless others did as well. I thought I was too far gone. Every time I walked into a room I felt uncomfortable; I felt as if I did not belong. Even when I would get dressed up for a family gathering or go out to a nice restaurant, I always felt that everyone could see right through me. Drug addict, drug dealer, degenerate gambler, criminal, all of the above. That must have been what they were thinking. I never wanted to associate with anyone who was not part of the insane lifestyle I was living.

Even when I tried to turn my life around and get out of that insane lifestyle, I kept getting sucked back in. The movies I watched and the music I listened to really did have a negative influence on my behavior as a kid. My brain on drugs fed on negativity. Just about everything I needed to hear to better myself went in one ear and out the other. Instead, I consumed everything that lead me down the wrong path. The criminal lifestyle is often glorified, and I fell into its embrace.

With the so many failed attempts at living a clean and sober life, my chances of success seemed hopeless. But every time I went into treatment or connected with another person in recovery, I took something away from that experience. Although my first inpatient stay was not a success, it helped me understand a little bit more about recovery the next time I went into treatment; the many times I went into treatment.

My family never gave up on me, especially my mom. They kept pushing for me to go back into treatment even when I had no interest in helping myself. But sometimes even wanting it for myself was not enough. On three separate occasions, I walked into an emergency room of my own accord asking to be admitted into the hospital's detox program, and all three times I was denied because I "did not meet the criteria for admission." I was using deadly amounts of opioids every single day. But even an everyday opioid abuser can sometimes test clean on a drug test after not using for as little as 24 hours. Insurance will only cover you in a detox if your urine is dirty and you are going through active withdrawals severe enough to "meet the criteria for admission." I even had one nurse tell me to go get high and come back so I could test dirty. That might sound insane, and it is, but the nurse who told me to do that had only the best intentions for me.

The entire admissions process into a detox which is based on "medical necessity" is a complete disaster. I know of a group that helps people get into detox by getting them drunk and giving them a small amount of Xanax so they will test positive for benzodiazepines on a drug test. The withdrawals from alcohol and benzodiazepines such as Xanax can be life threatening, so it is easier to get into a detox when someone tests positive for those drugs. For an opioid abuser, you might feel like you are going to die when going through withdrawals, but you won't. Instead, an opioid abuser will just go get high to stop the sickness, and possibly die from an overdose instead.

If the alcohol and Xanax strategy fails, then this group will instruct individuals to tell the nurses and doctors in the emergency room that they are having trouble breathing and have chest pains. If that fails, just tell the hospital employees that you are going to kill yourself.

I cannot condone this strategy because it is illegal and can sometimes turn ugly, but can you blame people for taking such drastic measures to try and save someone's life?

I hear many people say things such as, "They need to hit rock bottom," or, "They have to want it for themselves." To an extent, I disagree. When I arrived at Turning Point, I had no idea if I hit rock bottom, and I certainly did not want sobriety for myself. The only thing that got me in the door was the criminal justice system. If I never got arrested, I believe I never would have stopped living that insane lifestyle, and I would have never made it out of my twenties alive.

Expecting someone who just came off a run of abusing drugs to want sobriety for himself and to be certain he has hit "rock bottom" is both ridiculous and unrealistic. Was I thinking clearly on day 1 after years of abusing opioids? Absolutely not. Was I thinking clearly on day 30? Not a chance. It took me 6 months before I realized that I woke up and drugs was not the first thing on my mind. No matter where I was or how high or drunk I got the night before, my thought process was exactly the same each morning. Do I have drugs? If I do, okay. If not, how am I going to get them?

As word of mouth and social media started to spread about *Speak Sobriety*, I began to get more phone calls from people who had loved ones suffering from the disease of addiction. I have even received phone calls from parents who have lost their child to an overdose. The majority of the inquiries I get today are from parents who have a son or daughter suffering from opioid addiction. This type of phone call has become all too common for me.

Most of the time, their loved one has failed at treatment multiple times and there are usually criminal charges pending. Families come to me and they are lost. This is when I decided to implement treatment planning and interventions as part of *Speak Sobriety*.

My parents and I made many mistakes trying to get help. Some people are under the impression that sending their loved one, who is suffering from addiction, to a top of the line treatment facility for 1 month is going to be the cure. This could not be further from the truth, especially for opioid addiction.

Just think about it logically. When someone abuses opioids for years, what makes you think he or she can beat that habit in 1 month? In my opinion, more important than anything in treatment, is time. I would almost always rather send someone to a state facility for 90 days over an expensive private facility for 30 days. The problem is that the majority of people cannot afford to send their loved ones to extended care. It is hard enough dealing with insurance companies that don't want to pay even for inpatient treatment. Extended care is considered residential treatment and insurance companies will not cover any of those costs.

With the professional relationships I have with multiple reputable treatment facilities, I am able to help people come up with a long term treatment plan that will provide the best chance of long term recovery. I find ways to help families stretch their funds to keep their loved ones in treatment for as long as possible.

Eventually, I had to want sobriety for myself. That comes with time. What I got most out of Turning Point was the camaraderie of being in an environment with sober men who all suffered from the same disease and were trying to stay sober one day at a time. There is nothing that compares to the support I received, and still get, from my peers in recovery. We understand each other through our common struggle. I never feel alone or different when I am around my friends in recovery. There are things I can say to them that I cannot say to anyone else. They just get it.

Some of the friendships I made in my journey to recovery will last a lifetime. I was with Eric from pretty much every day for the first 2 years of my recovery. Bill came in later, but I am just as close with him today.

Just as important as the treatment of addiction is prevention. This is why I started speaking at schools. More than just exposing the horrors of addiction, *Speak Sobriety* is about highlighting the benefits of living a clean and sober lifestyle.

The "War on Drugs" approach has been an epic failure. When America decided to declare war on drugs, we declared war on ourselves. No matter what measures we take, drugs will always find a way into this country. As long as there is still a need for drugs, dealers will always surface to serve those needs. It's as simple as supply and demand. Until the culture around drugs and alcohol changes, this horrible disease will continue to take the lives of Americans at a horrifying rate.

My disease of addiction and my life experience as a result of my actions have been both a blessing and a curse. But the curse for me is over, and today I use my experiences as a blessing. I have been given a chance to use my struggles to prevent someone else from making the same mistakes I did. I am able to give hope to those who feel as helpless as I did during the height of my addiction.

With that being said, I must stay vigilant in my recovery. I cannot afford to get complacent and think to myself, "I got this." I have heard stories of people relapsing after having over a decade of clean time. I have to protect my recovery at all costs. People, places, and things are so important for me. If I am hanging out late at a college bar with people who are blackout drunk and snorting cocaine, I have done something terribly wrong. I go to great lengths to make sure I do not expose myself to certain situations. Sometimes, it becomes a burden. But that burden is part of my blessing as it enables me to help others.

Even with all the planning I do to protect my recovery, sometimes, life just happens. I have had two major events occur while in recovery, and they could have ended up being major setbacks. People's sobriety is at risk no matter how much clean time they have, or work they have put into their recovery.

The first event happened in July of 2015 when I had major back surgery. I had a herniated disc that was causing excruciating pain, so I had no choice but to go under the knife. I told my doctor that I was a recovering addict and that opioid painkillers were my drug of choice. He thanked me for my honesty, and told me that I would be in a lot of pain for the first few days after my surgery, so I would need to take painkillers.

My disease was thrilled by the doctor's remarks. My heart started to race, my eyes were watery, I clenched my fists and grinded my teeth. This was the feeling of the high before the high. Some addicts will tell you that the anticipation of getting high is better than the high itself.

Over the next few weeks, I found myself looking forward to surgery so I could take painkillers. It was a constant battle in my head: addiction vs. recovery, good vs. evil, right vs. wrong. I knew how insane my thoughts were, so instead of keeping those thoughts to myself, I talked openly about them with other men in my sober network.

After my surgery, the doctor prescribed a six-day supply of painkillers. I gave the prescription to my mother and girlfriend to hold onto. After three days of taking 5mg Oxycodone pills, I told my mother to get rid of them. I couldn't tell if I actually needed the pain killers because of the pain from my surgery, or if my disease was convincing me that I needed them. It became overwhelming and I started to get really scared.

I had multiple people in recovery checking up on me every day after my surgery. A few of my friends from Turning Point and the New Haven recovery community came to visit me at my parent's house. I know how lucky I am to have such an amazing family and recovery support system. I could not have made it through without them.

The second major event completely changed my story. I had to delete and rewrite the last chapter and a half of this book just days before I was ready to publish. The deleted portion was all about my relationship with a girl I met just weeks after I moved back to my parents' house in August of 2014. We dated for over 3 years, and she was the love of my life, or so I thought.

In the deleted chapters, I talked about how amazing our relationship was and how she was the greatest gift of my sobriety. We got engaged in May of 2017. About a week after our engagement party in July of 2017, right before I was about to start my first semester of law school, I got a call from my friend Dale asking me to come to his new house. I was close by, so I headed right over. When I arrived at Dale's house, I knew he was about to tell me something horrible just by the look on his face. Dale found out my fiancé was having an affair, and he broke the news to me. I had suspected it for a while, but just didn't think that could happen to us. I just kept saying to myself, "She would never do that to me." I was wrong.

Dale and I went through Turning Point together. He was one of my closest friends there. Dale was so scared to tell me because he was seriously concerned about how I would react. The first thing Dale said to me after he broke the awful news to me was, "Please don't get high Steve, I will stay with you for as long as you need me to, just please don't get high." Words cannot describe how much respect I gained for Dale on that day, and how grateful I am to have him as a friend.

My life struggles have made me an understanding and forgiving person, so I gave my fiancé another chance. She cheated again, or likely never stopped. I had no choice but to break off our engagement just weeks after we had sent out our save the date cards.

Relationships and broken hearts are one of the leading causes of relapse. This is why it is recommended to stay out of a relationship for the first year of sobriety. To say that I did not think about getting high during the hardest days of my recovery would be a lie. But I used my support system to help me get through those tough times. I talked with my family, sponsor, and other men in my sober network every day and these discussions helped me remain a sober man. Absolutely nothing is worth throwing away my sobriety.

I understand fully the risks of publishing my memoir that shares some of the most intimate details of my life in addiction and recovery. I was hesitant to write it at first, but then my former SAT tutor, Marc Hoberman, convinced me. He found out about Speak Sobriety when he was helping my younger brother with a college essay. We reconnected, and Marc came to see me speak at Suffern High School. He came up to me after my presentation with tears in his eyes and said, "You have to write a book; your story can help countless people." So, I did just that. It was easy for me to trust Marc and work with him because he also suffers from a disease, epilepsy. I read Marc's memoir *Adversity Defeated: Turn Your Struggles into Strengths*, and understood why I was meant to share my story in the same way.

If my honesty prevents me from getting a job, furthering my career, or causes someone to judge me or look down on me, then so be it. To me, it has already been worth it. I have a mission and a passion, and I will see it through until the end. I have emerged from a great darkness, and I am alive for a reason, and *Speak Sobriety* is that reason.

Gateway Drugs

The Gateway drug debate will likely never end. Those who believe marijuana and alcohol are not gateway drugs have an agenda, as do those who say that marijuana and alcohol are gateway drugs. I have read numerous studies and talked with countless addicts, recreational drinkers and smokers, and those who work in the field of addiction. In the end, I firmly believe that marijuana and alcohol ARE gateway drugs, for SOME people.

In all my years with experience in active addiction and in recovery, I have never met someone who is or was addicted to heroin who did not start out with marijuana. Never. I believe marijuana is a gateway drug more for behavioral reasons, and alcohol more for the state of mind that a drunk person is put in. I will start with marijuana.

The first time someone smokes pot is usually in their teens. No teenager takes their first hit with the intention of becoming addicted to marijuana, or to start down a road to harder drugs like narcotic painkillers or heroin. Some teens will try it once or a few times, and never pick it up again. Others will smoke occasionally throughout high school and maybe college, and then phase it out of their lives as they get older. Some however, will become habitual marijuana smokers. It starts with "I'm just going to try it this once." That one time turns into a second. The second time turns into "I am just going to smoke weed on the weekends."

Then, you smoke once during the week too. Before you know it, you are smoking every day. Later on, an opportunity presents itself. Maybe someone stole a prescription for Xanax from their mom. Maybe someone got their wisdom teeth pulled and brought a prescription for

Oxycodone to a party. That same teen tries it with the intention of only